Journeys in Dust and Light

A Modern Pilgrimage
Through the Life and Letters of Paul

John DeMers

A Michael Glazier Book
THE LITURGICAL PRESS
Collegeville, Minnesota

A Michael Glazier Book published by The Liturgical Press

Cover design by David Manahan, O.S.B.
Cover photograph courtesy of Turkish Ministry of Tourism.
Interior photographs by John DeMers.

1   2   3   4   5   6   7   8   9

Library of Congress Cataloging-in-Publication Data

DeMers, John, 1952–
    Journeys in dust and light : a modern pilgrimage through the life and letters of Paul / John DeMers.
        p.   cm.
    Includes bibliographical references.
    ISBN 0-8146-5701-X
    1. Paul, the Apostle, Saint—Journeys. 2. Bible. N.T.
Epistles of Paul—Criticism, interpretation, etc.   3. Mediterranean Region—Description and travel.   I. Title.
BS2506.D45   1993
227'.091—dc20   92-40482
                                                          CIP

To SANDRA,
SARA, MICHAEL, AMANDA
and TESSA

Who made this journey in my heart

We even boast of our afflictions, knowing that affliction produces endurance, and endurance, proven character, and proven character, hope, and hope does not disappoint because the love of God has been poured out into our hearts.

Romans 5:3-6

Contents

Roman Stones in Philippi

1

SALUTATION

Paul, a slave of Christ Jesus, called to be an apostle and set apart for the gospel of God, which was promised previously through the prophets in the holy scriptures, the gospel about God's son. . . . Grace to you and peace from God our Father and the Lord Jesus Christ!

Romans 1:1-7

All Christendom knows the apostle Paul as a determined and tireless traveler, one whose thirteen thousand miles were amassed nearly two millennia before airlines and frequent flyer awards made accumulation both painless and artificial. Yet what Paul was like as a traveling companion remained a mystery to me—until I allowed his tumultuous life and letters to dictate an itinerary through Israel, Turkey, Greece, and Italy.

His companionship, by any human measure, was second-hand. I traveled with a knowledge of the route he had taken, spreading the good news of God's saving action. And I traveled with a copy of his letters, which make up a significant portion of what Christians call the New Testament. What I did not have was a certain or even probable sense of Paul himself.

I had no vision of Paul physically, despite the thousands of renderings in churches throughout the world. In all of these two thousand years, it seems, there is only one description of how he actually looked, and that not even in Scripture. More than a century after his death someone set down a memory of spotting Paul on the royal road to Lystra near Iconium. It must not have been one of Paul's better days: "A man small in size, with a bald head, and bowlegged, strongly built, with eyebrows meeting and a somewhat hooked and large nose." He walked with a noticeable limp. In terms of appearance, this is not a flattering legacy. Yet his legacy is considerably larger than the body he saw only as metaphor for a grander, more life-giving unity. The same work, The Acts of Paul and Thecla, recalls that "he was full of grace, for at times he looked like a man, at times like an angel."

For all his road-hardened determination, reflected no doubt in the phrase "strongly built," Paul was perhaps the ultimate "accidental tourist"—a traveler who abandoned his itinerary without apology at the suggestion of voices and visions. He spoke often of the Spirit who made his travel plans, and he labored lifelong toward obedience in this, as in all things. Yet Paul was also the first true business traveler, ever ready to retrace his steps to seal a deal negotiated earlier. When he could not get away, he wrote. But quite often, Scripture assures us, he got away. As a result, the crisscrossed routes of his missionary journeys bankrupt the powers of an earthly travel agent and exhaust the resources of any would-be traveler. A single westward assault would have to suffice for me, one that reflected as best it could the biography and the theology of Paul.

There were and are many reasons for following in the footsteps of Paul. Wherever he turns up in Scripture, things start to happen. In Acts of the Apostles, for instance, the author introduces Paul to Antioch and only then lets on that in this city followers of Jesus were first known as Christians. This gives us no proof that Paul coined the term; yet in light of the author's awkward sequence and Paul's later reputation, it is likely his teachings made it clear the fledgling Church in Antioch was no mere sect of Judaism.

It was Paul, too, in letter after passionate letter, who filled out the theology of Jesus. Writing before a single gospel was set down, Paul outlined with dazzling insight nearly every major theological concept studied, debated, and embraced by Christians to this day. Beginning time and again with ideas encountered on the road to becoming a rabbi, Paul exploded them inward and outward with the light he encountered on a different road: the one that led to Damascus. God's presence, God's power, God's fidelity, God's forgiveness, God's vindication, God's love—each of these concepts and a dozen more Paul transformed from a single-minded testimonial to one chosen people into God's all-gathering embrace of the earth and all who are upon it.

In this transformation, it was no one but the Jew born Saul who took hold of Christianity and turned it forever toward the West. In body, he pushed onto European soil and preached the good news of Jesus. In mind and spirit, he formed from Hellenistic Roman thought a form of missionary Judaism the world had not seen and was not to see again. Missionary Judaism seemed a contradiction to Paul and to most who heard him preach; yet no more a contradiction than a king who came as a slave, or a death that ushered humanity into life.

Still, for each of these reasons for seeking Paul, there seemed a dozen painful questions demanding to be asked. In the end, the reasons were insufficient to compel my journey— to tear me away from my pregnant wife, trio of young children, and unforgiving fulltime job. The questions proved irresistible.

Was Paul, for instance, the chosen theologian of Jesus the Messiah, selected from eternity to spin concept upon concept from a handful of parables told by a carpenter's son? Or was he a dreary and dangerous falsifier who buried whatever we might have known of Jesus under cosmic constructions that the simple teacher from Nazareth would not have even recognized? Was Paul the hate-filled former Jew who drove a wedge between his old people and his new, giving all Christian generations the alleged blessing of their God on anti-Semitism? Or was he the faithful seed of Abraham to the end, praying when all other prayers ran dry that God would draw finally into the kingdom the original people to whom the king-dom had been revealed?

Was Paul the apostle of unity, seeing all creation in one crust of bread and one cup of wine, inviting Gentile and Jew, slave and free, woman and man into union with one Lord? Or was he the ultimate divider, the "father of all heresies," whose anthems are sung any and every time one Christian sect removes itself in anger from another? "Is Christ divided?" Paul would ask at one point in his ministry. Is it because of Paul, we might ask, that the answer so often seems "Yes"?

And finally, was Paul the studious architect of Church as we know it, that time-tangled gathering of heavenly gifts and spirit-filled job descriptions, empowered to complete the work of Jesus on earth? Or was he the frenzied prophet of yet another would-be apocalypse, trudging the backroads of Pax Romana proclaiming in vain that the end was near? Or again, as I hoped against hope when beginning my own back-road journey, was he a visionary to whom the coming triumph of God seemed so immediate, so intense, so personal that he could breathe blood and heart and bones and brains and life and love into the Church when it knew their dimensions so scantily—a visionary who can and should and must breathe these qualities into us once again?

Question crowded upon question as I took my first halt-ing steps into Paul's time and place, into a world choked with dust from crumbling columns, a world of cities whose ancient names are not even known by those who live within them. Yet, I had faith that there were answers waiting to be found. These, I knew, were hidden among the rocks and brambles, like so many truths among Paul's own feverish punctuation. Deep within me, the conviction grew that somewhere in Paul's life of journeys, whole or in a thousand scattered pieces, lay the map of my future life.

In the Tiny Museum of Tarsus

2

TARSUS

*I am a Jew, of Tarsus in Cilicia, a citizen of no mean
city; I request you to permit me to speak to the people.*
                                                    Acts 21:39

*Many are the plans in a man's heart, but it is the decision
of the Lord that endures.*
                                               Proverbs 19:21

The bus making the run from the Turkish industrial hub
of Adana to the busy port of Mersin little more than stuttered
as it deposited me at the side of the highway. Darkness had
fallen, with a vengeance it seemed, or perhaps there were
simply no street lights; and the driver's only response to my
queries about where he was leaving me was a wave attached
to the briefest of smiles.

"Tarsus," he said finally, shutting the door with a rush
of released air, and gunning the bus toward Mersin.

Tarsus! I had arrived in the city of Paul's birth, the city
of his earliest education in the ways of both God and the world.
Yet, I must admit that in my briefest of introductions to this
once-significant city, I feared that both God and world had
abandoned it long before I stood at the side of its one reason-
ably good highway. In the deep purple darkness, I could hear
horses' hooves and carriage wheels, broken now and again
by the unmuffled roar of a truck or motorcycle. And as my
eyes adjusted to the low light, I decided I liked Tarsus better
when I couldn't see.

At every turn there were broken fences and rusty tin
roofs, hastily assembled carts leaning against walls on one

wheel, and ramshackle shops devoted to a thousand tasks that all resembled carburetor repair. The heat was oppressive in the night, a wet and sticky swamp heat that grew worse as I shouldered my duffle bag, picked a street with a lifeless prayer, and started into Paul's hometown.

Within an hour of walking, I had followed several sets of directions toward a near-mythical Hotel Zorbas that everyone agreed was the best in town. One shopkeeper, who admittedly had moved to Tarsus from Ankara only six months before, described the Zorbas as absolutely "luks." And while pampering seldom tops my list of travel needs, I was already feeling a desperate longing for separation from the Tarsus I was encountering. Perhaps, as ever hoped in the wanderer's favorite phrase, everything would look friendlier in the morning.

Sadly, the shopkeeper's directions were so tangled that a taxi had to retrace all my steps plus some to reach the Luks Hotel Zorbas. And my deluxe room five flights up proved to be a hot, airless cell with just one window letting in the growls of what seemed the busiest nocturnal market street in Tarsus. I lay sweating atop the covers, realizing that for all the times I'd seen it in movies, I'd never before tried to sleep in a room painted red by neon. And I tried to remember why, in all my foolishness, I had ever thought it worth leaving home, wife, and children to seek a person dead nearly two thousand years in a city that seemed equally decomposed.

> *For we are God's handiwork, created in Christ Jesus for the good works that God has prepared in advance, that we should live in them.*
>
> Ephesians 2:10

During that hot, sleepless night in Tarsus, there were many things to ponder, and they all converged suddenly on the word "accident." Forgetting with effort the accident of my being here, there was the accident of the city's geography as bridge between east and west. There was the accident of its favored position in the Greek and Roman worlds, one that made it a center of education, rivaling even Athens and Alexandria. There was the accident of its Jews in residence, at least some of whom received Roman citizenship from Julius Caesar himself. And there were the thousand other accidents of life and death—those that make us male or female, rich or poor, slave or free, tentmaker or carpenter's son. Pondering the Tarsus that formed a Jew named Saul, is was clear that in God's history there are no accidents.

King Midas of Phrygia, Cyrus and Darius of Persia, Alexander the Great, Julius Caesar, Antony and Cleopatra—all these figures and more left their seemingly unlikely imprints upon Tarsus. Scripture also added a stroke or two, its "sons of Javan," possibly referring to Ionian traders in the region (Gen 10:4), and the Old Testament's "Tarshish" believably being Tarsus (Ezek 27:12; Jer 10:9). As described in these later references, silver, iron, and lead did indeed pass through the city on their way to Tyre by sea.

By the third century before Christ, Tarsus was a vigorous business center ten miles from the Mediterranean, clinging to the last straight strip before the land slipped down toward what today is Israel by way of Syria and Lebanon. Even in its earliest days, summers here were oppressive, inspiring citizens of the settlement known then as Kodrigai to build a second, more comfortable version of itself a few miles north. With its summer resort bringing better conditions and its warm, moist air bringing agricultural success, Tarsus prospered early in its special place on the Cydnus River at the edge of the Cilician Plain. Its population climbed to over 500,000 at one point.

A mere twenty-two miles to the north were the fabled Cilician Gates, a narrow pathway through the Taurus Mountains, offering the only safe access from Europe and Asia Minor to Palestine and the ancient lands of the Tigris and

Euphrates. A profitable east-west trade developed over the centuries, using either the "land bridge" that curved down around the Mediterranean or the harbor dredged by visionary Tarsians from a swamp rimmed with sand dunes. Through the harbor town of Aulai, merchandise arrived in Tarsus from all over the ancient world.

Generally, the people of Tarsus identified their origins among the "Sea Peoples" who settled in the Cilician Plain around 1200 B.C., as well as among Mycenean refugees from the Trojan War. From the start, Tarsus displayed nothing less than a brilliance for accommodation, adjusting in succession to rule by Cilicians, Hittites, Assyrians, Phrygians, and Persians. Alexander the Great entered the city in 334 B.C. after it and its Persian overlords had offered only token resistance. Residents clearly had taken to heart the inscription on one of their favorite Assyrian monuments: "Eat, drink and be merry; for all else is worthless."

Alexander understood the strategic location of Tarsus every bit as well as the conquerors who had marched through before him, especially after his victory over Darius III at nearby Issos. Yet Alexander died that very year, leaving Tarsus to suffer through more than a century of anarchy as Seleucids and Ptolemies wrestled for the upper hand.

Dark days, however, have often pressed humanity toward deeper understanding of itself; and so it was in Tarsus. The city and its surrounding plain entered a golden age of philosophy and literature, even as and perhaps because its confidence in tomorrow sank so low. Chrysippus was the best-known of Zeno's successors as head of the Stoic school, a system of thought Tarsus' most famous son would later confront on the streets of Athens itself. Aratus penned poems about astronomy, while Philemon concentrated on comedy—a natural concentration in times of physical and spiritual danger.

In his famous *Geography*, Strabo expressed for all time the ancient world's esteem: "The people of Tarsus have devoted themselves so eagerly, not only to philosophy, but to the whole of education in general, that they have surpassed Athens, Alexandria, or any other place that can be named where there have been schools and lectures of philosophers.''

By the second century before Jesus' birth, it was Rome that recognized the value of this real estate, pushing down through Lydia, Phrygia, and Lycaonia until Tarsus became the frontier between Roman advance and Seleucid withdrawal. Tarsus proved capable of being friend to both sides, granting passage and a host of other favors in return for the one bribe it desired above all others, freedom. It grew during this period into the region's most powerful city, choosing its own officials, living by its own laws, even issuing its own coins.

When Rome finally did move in, as much to rid the eastern Mediterranean of pirates as to control the Cilician Plain, the people of Tarsus skillfully changed the game pieces without changing the game. Indeed, they discovered many advantages in belonging to Rome: peace, order, justice, and reasonable taxes. During his march from Egypt in 47 B.C., Julius Caesar met with provincial officials in Tarsus and, according to tradition, granted full citizenship to certain Tarsians who had served him well. Among these, tradition has it, was the grandfather of one ''of the race of Israel, of the tribe of Benjamin, a Hebrew of Hebrew parentage'' (Phil 3:5). In gratitude, the local citizenry renamed their city ''Juliopolis,'' if only temporarily.

Caesar's assassination in Rome thrust the empire into a dark and bloody period. Yet the survival skills of the city that shaped young Saul once again proved exemplary. An excruciating fine imposed by Cassius was quickly balanced by Mark Antony, who awarded Tarsus the honor of being a free city with self rule and duty-free trade. Antony, for his part, first met Cleopatra in the city after she had sailed up the Cydnus on her royal barge. Their disastrous love affair was ignited here, with the Egyptian queen seducing Antony into his campaign against Octavian. After victory at Actium in 31 B.C., Octavian proclaimed himself Augustus and claimed

sovereignty over the entire Roman world. For Tarsus, however, he added his imperial stamp to the privileges granted
by Antony.

Once again, in a memory certain to be fresh in the streets
walked by young Saul, Tarsus had done what Tarsus did best.
It had been Greek to the Greeks, Persian to the Persians, now
Roman to the Romans. It had been, quite to its own delight,
all things to all people.

> *As the two walked on together, Isaac spoke to his father*
> *Abraham. "Father!" he said. "Yes, son," he replied. Isaac*
> *continued, "Here are the fire and the wood, but where is the*
> *sheep for the holocaust?" "Son," Abraham answered, "God*
> *will provide the sheep for the holocaust."*
>
> Genesis 22:7-8

Tarsus did look friendlier in the morning, if only slightly
more photogenic. Shopkeepers with water buckets and make-
shift brooms splashed the sidewalks in hopes the dust would
stay down. Horse carts delivered the makings of commerce,
from bundles of twigs to greased engine parts. And tiny boys
darted in and out of doorways, balancing trays of fresh-baked
sesame rings on their heads, calling out "Simit! Simit!" to
all who might need a bit of breakfast. I was hungry only for
Saul; yet I was beginning to fear there would be no breakfast
and it was a long time until lunch.

Breezing through Tarsus' Pauline "sites" proved virtually unavoidable. The city's only true landmark, identified
in literature as "St. Paul's Gate," turned out to be Cleopatra's
Gate in actuality. The name didn't matter much, considering that the hulking stone archway in the center of a busy
street clearly dated from centuries too late to belong to either
illustrious chapter in Tarsian history. Far more meaningful
was the simple stone well, now encircled by a fence with daily

hours of admission, identified since antiquity as belonging to Saul's birthplace.

As elsewhere in the biblical world, we can choose to scoff at such traditions; yet we can also choose not to scoff, recognizing the persuasiveness of identifications made so close to a date we cannot reach in any other way. The worn gray stones seemed testimony enough for the moment; though perhaps I was hearing the testimonies of so many centuries that believed in them.

Suddenly it seemed I had exhausted Tarsus, that the remaining hours of my visit had no purpose. I walked in broad, expanding circles around the city center, skirting and then exploring neighborhoods that had little to recommend them. It was one of these slow, careless loops that carried me into the heart of Saul's Tarsus.

There, just a brisk walk past the old Turkish bath and in the shadow of a mosque's mud-brown minaret, was the city's tiny museum, no more than a courtyard, with only a sprinkling of pieces from the past. Still, the sprinkling was what I had been unknowingly searching for, a doorway out of Tarsus now and into Tarsus then. I realized quickly, catching the occasional swirl of Judaica among the stones crammed with Greek and Latin characters, that I was failing to find Saul precisely because I was seeking one person. What I had to look for always, I knew from this moment on, was three.

At every crucial turn of his life Saul of Tarsus was simultaneously a Greek, a Roman, and a Jew. I stood breathlessly among the stones, with only a guard dozing behind his mustache for company, pondering what it must have meant to one young man walking these streets to be Greek in thought, Roman in vision, and Jewish in faith.

To be a Greek thinker in Saul's day was, above all, to believe in thinking. The splendor that was Greece was only a memory, yet the spirit of that splendor lived on in Tarsus' reverence for education, for wit, for reason. In particular, Saul learned from the world that encircled him not only the versatility of the Greek language but the subtleties of statement and argument that had been the lifeblood of Athens in its day. Later, confronting his opponents in city after city—and nowhere more than in cities full of Greeks—Saul would resort to the same techniques used by Socrates and, no doubt, by a host of latter-day imitators in the marketplace of Tarsus.

To be a Roman visionary in Saul's day was, above all, to believe in vision. The empire had been built on vision, rising as it had from a scattering of hill-settlements to encompass the entire Mediterranean world. Unique in human history, this global kingdom was constructed not on a land or a race or a culture, but on the dazzling power of a single city. And the peace delivered by its power was an awesome thing indeed. To a young Roman citizen like Saul, Pax Romana meant the entire world lay before him—a world of mountain roads cleared of bandits and sea lanes purged of pirates, a world of linguistic and monetary exchange, a world with a solid and magnetic core. There was no room for thinking small in such a world.

Finally, to be a Jewish believer in Saul's day was, above all, to believe in belief. It is clear that Saul was a Jew above all else, holding fast to the traditions of his people. Even his name was an act of tradition, linking him to Saul, the first king of Israel and the most famous member of Benjamin's tribe. As a child of such orthodox faith, and indeed a child sent to Jerusalem for rabbinical studies, Saul knew well the history of God and God's chosen people. He knew, from tireless instruction, the story of this love affair sealed by the law of Moses and shaken with regularity by the people's refusal to live by the law. Yet he knew too of God's abiding love, love that took the form of a promise to a man named Abraham who believed. On that day, from this belief, a people was formed for God's purpose, and another, even larger promise was made.

Standing among the museum's stones, I could not help wondering what Saul thought as he prepared to leave Tarsus for his studies in Jerusalem. Did he think of this promise at all, a promise that made his a people in waiting? Did he, as a young Jew of Greek thought and Roman vision, wonder about this God the conqueror? Did he envision God's empire as small and select, like Athens, the envy of all but the possession of few? Or could he glimpse the distant outlines of an empire that reached beyond the mountains and seas, to lands untouched even by Rome? Might this conqueror, in some new way, follow Alexander, Caesar, and all others before him, making Tarsus his bridge among the peoples?

It is conceivable that Saul entertained such thoughts—as a Tarsian, how could he not?—perhaps during a hot and sleepless night before departing. It is even conceivable that he wondered what small role he might play in God's conquest. Perhaps he might help design such a bridge, or construct such a bridge, or explain such a bridge with erudition in the synagogue. Yet even on the hottest and most sleepless of nights, it is unlikely Saul realized he would be that bridge, building up, then laying down his life that God the conqueror might cross.

Excavations of Roman Jerusalem

3

JERUSALEM

I am the least of the apostles, unfit to be called an apostle,
because I persecuted the Church of God. But by the grace of God
I am what I am, and God's grace to me has not been ineffective.
I Corinthians 15:9

Therefore, we are children not of the slave woman but of
the freeborn woman. For freedom Christ set us free; so stand firm
and do not submit again to the yoke of slavery.
Galatians 4:31-5:1

The taxi sputtered to a stop at the barricade and, rolling down his window, my driver embarked on a brief but feverish exchange in Hebrew with the stiff-standing policeman. The driver's hands lifted from the wheel in frustration, then settled back down in surrender to the inevitable. He ground the taxi into reverse, backed too fast down a long residential block and started by a different route into the ancient, inspiring, ever-troubling city of Jerusalem.

"It is the Sabbath," he explained to me, once he had rolled up the window so we could enjoy the air conditioning. "It is," he struggled for the word in English, "some extremists. You know, some very orthodox. They say we should not drive on the Sabbath. It is nothing. But if we are seen driving in their neighborhood, they will throw at us perhaps some stones."

I did not realize it at that moment, but even before I entered the physical heart of Jerusalem, I was entering its spiritual heart. I knew I was searching for Saul in the holy city of David and Jesus, searching for a man who, like both of them, had been born a Jew. I figured I would know him when I saw him, in all his ferocious Jewishness, perhaps striding through some dusty gate or arguing the law from some toppled Roman column. I could only glimpse the truth at the time, but I first sensed Saul in Jerusalem at that Sabbath-silent police barricade.

The fact is, Paul the Apostle is a mere shadow in the city. He seems on permanent leave from its otherwise substantial dust and memory, its tangled streets and covered passageways. Jesus is everywhere in Jerusalem, as man of history, God of faith and drawing card of tourism. Yet Paul has been banished, his footsteps covered over by time and purpose, as though for two thousand years of Jerusalem's life his preaching has been more scandalous than even the cross he preached. It was clear from the start that this was no accident, just as it was clear that in these now-foreign streets I was called to realize Saul the Jew could become Paul the Christian, but could never leave behind his lineage, his heritage, or his identity.

Jerusalem, for all its unexpected beauty—its thousand shades of stone sprouting patches of green, its sun-burnished towers and golden domes—would become for Saul a city in chains, in chains to the very religion that sang serenades to freedom from slavery and to return from exile. For me, seeking Saul's memory, Jerusalem would remain a city in chains, from the Arab shopkeepers shut down by PLO extortion to the Christian factions battling over turf to the Orthodox Jews throwing stones on the Sabbath. These were the very chains, I came to realize, that Paul devoted his life to breaking. He devoted his life to breaking them, paradoxically, with the deepest conviction that the One with whom his life would collide had broken them already.

*For you heard of my former way of life in Judaism, how
I persecuted the Church of God beyond measure and tried to de-*

stroy it, and progressed in Judaism beyond many of my contem-
poraries among my race, for I was a zealot for my ancestral
traditions.

Galatians 1:13

I stood at the center of the modern causeway leading into
the Old City through the Damascus Gate, an unadorned
bridge that carried me into the dark mouth of Jerusalem's
most extraordinary piece of Islamic architecture. Even in the
pink dusk, I could pick out the different colors of stone, and
I could concentrate on them now that the golden Dome of
the Rock and the gray dome of the Holy Sepulchre had fallen
behind the ornate Ottoman wall. There were many shades,
from almost white to dark gray-brown, some no doubt from
as late as 1967, when the gate was rescued from disrepair.
Yet for all the Arab, Crusader, and Turkish dominance in
this corner of Jerusalem, I was struck most by what I saw
while glancing down from the causeway into the shadows.
There, lying as though in a coma without memory, were stones
from the Roman city of Saul.

The city the young man from Tarsus explored whenever
he wasn't studying or praying was a world apart from Jerusalem today. It shimmered in the sun, we are told, with the glory
of Greece by way of Rome—a new and seemingly eternal glory
that for Saul must have been as exhilarating as it was scandalous. To the west, near what is today the Jaffa Gate, Herod
the Great had built three magnificent towers and a new palace, one used by procurators such as Pontius Pilate, and even
by Herod Agrippa during his three-year reign.

It is difficult to remember that Caesarea on the coast was
the capital at that time, difficult, that is, until we visit the dramatic excavations there of a grand Roman city gazing confi-
dently across the Mediterranean to the heart of the Roman
world. Yet Jerusalem, then as now, was Palestine's city of
holiness. Saul in particular must have sensed not only the
whole of Palestine and Syria yearning to walk its often-blessed

streets, but the whole of the earth, wherever there were Jews driven or drawn, wherever there were Jews struggling to remember.

The center of Saul's life, especially as a teenager sent by his parents to become a rabbi, must have been the resplendent Temple constructed by Herod on a dizzying platform across the city's heights. Saul also would have been quite familiar, as a Roman, with the Antonia Fortress on Temple Mount, four thick towers and a courtyard that housed a garrison standing ready to quell any Jewish insurrections. And Saul no doubt knew well Herod's theater, hippodrome and amphitheater, which had so offended his Jewish subjects. It was such offenses that put the Antonia garrison to work regularly, as the time when zealots rioted and cut down an eagle placed by Herod over one of the Temple entrances in defiance of Mosaic law. Saul would have thought of such conflicts—conflicts he knew to some degree within himself—as he gazed at the Antonia. He could not have known he would be imprisoned in this same fortress a lifetime later, instigator and victim of a conflict he could not begin to foresee.

Today, just as Paul would eventually view his quarrel not with flesh and blood but with "principalities and powers," Saul's Jerusalem is found not in stone and marble but in words and ideas. We sense his presence most vividly here when we encounter words we as Christians presume we understand: words like covenant, fidelity, Sabbath, circumcision, atonement, law. We know these are words Saul not only learned early and pondered long but used until the day he died. He may have expanded or even exploded them in directions unforeseen, but they remained the vessel that reverently held his new vision of God.

Yet what was Saul's "old" vision? In the deepest sense, it no more became obsolete to him in a single moment than the so-called Old Testament became obsolete with the writing and gathering of the New. What kind of Jew was Saul? And what better place than Jerusalem to pursue answers to such a question?

Jews Praying at the Western Wall

First, we cannot call even this "Hebrew born of Hebrews" (Phil 3:5) a Jew and let it go at that. Within Judaism, then as now, there were myriad formations and colorations of belief, just as there were and are among Christians. Paul tells us much when he reveals he was a Pharisee, and we know it was to Gamaliel and other members of that sect that he was sent from Tarsus to study. All these years removed from Saul's world, we are likely to stumble over the seeming familiarity of the Pharisees, seeing only the one praying boastfully in the synagogue while the publican prays humbly at the door, recalling only that it was Pharisees who pushed Jesus through the Roman legal system to the cross. Yet, if there were ever a group that could complain of "bad press," it is the Pharisees. We see, with no small amount of surprise, that of the three major factions of Judaism in Saul's lifetime, Pharisees had the most in common with the teachings of Jesus.

Saul was clearly no Sadducee, the aristocratic caste within which the high priests of the Temple were chosen from the reign of Solomon up to the time of the Maccabees. Though they functioned primarily as a Jewish ruling class, they did have a theological underpinning: a strict reading of the Scriptures that allowed little compromise with oral law and other developments over the centuries. They were, therefore, highly suspicious of the Pharisees, along with their adoption of newer faith components such as angels and the resurrection.

Saul was clearly no Essene, a still-mysterious sect known to us primarily from the first-century writings of Philo of Alexandria and Flavius Josephus. Under the banner "hasidim" (or "pious ones"), these believers cut themselves off from Jerusalem and lived as outcasts from one ritual to the next. We meet the Essenes in the eerie caves of Qumran along the Dead Sea, and particularly in the scrolls discovered in one such cave in 1947. As displayed in Jerusalem's Shrine of the Book, the Dead Sea Scrolls reveal a people apocalyptic to the extreme, seeking to live the holiest lives while awaiting one final battle between the "sons of darkness" and the "sons of light." Scriptural promises notwithstanding, these particular "sons of light" lost their final battle, though darkness took the form of Roman soldiers. The Essenes disappeared from Judaism and from history after hiding their beloved scrolls. It is often suggested that John the Baptist was an Essene. While Christians honor him primarily as herald of the Messiah—"a voice of one crying out in the desert, 'Prepare the way of the Lord.' '' (Luke 3:4-5)—there is nothing in what we know of John's life or thought that would disqualify him.

Yes, in telling us he was a Pharisee, Paul is telling us quite a lot, even considering the significant differences between him and his own teacher, Gamaliel. For starters, he is telling us that he, along with Sadducees and Essenes, saw the primary actor in human history as God. All history, therefore, spoke to Saul of God's work on behalf of humankind— nearly always as that great spiritual pendulum of God's fidelity and human infidelity, God's love and what was seen clearly as human sin. Yet as a Pharisee, Saul came to define sin in a very precise way, as failure to obey the law; and he came to view that law as a tangle of rule and ritual demanding tireless, arguably fanatical care. It was on this issue—no small thing ultimately, describing as it did what God wants— that the Pharisees embarked on their collision course with Jesus.

The teacher from Nazareth did not speak against the law itself or call for its dismantling. "I have come," he said, "not to abolish but to fulfill" (Matt 5:17-20). Yet his reordering of priorities, giving God and people a more direct relationship, was inevitably an affront to anyone who lived by ritual. His association with the lost, the weak and the sinful was an insult beyond toleration, even for Pharisees who knew their Messiah would come "to bring glad tidings to the lowly, to heal the brokenhearted, to proclaim liberty to the captives and release to the prisoners" (Isa 61:1; Luke 7:22). And his many works on the Sabbath infuriated any Pharisee as deadly threats to the perceived order of things. The law brought order and order was the law; yet Jesus portrayed this Pharisaic law as nothing short of slavery. It was a slavery Saul the Pharisee

2,000-Year-Old Olive Trees on
the Mount of Olives

would embrace in heart-stopping detail. It was a slavery that Paul the Apostle would declare at its end.

For God who said, "Let the light shine out of darkness," has shown in our hearts to bring the light of knowledge of the glory of God on the face of Christ.

II Corinthians 4:6

There are few places, really, for us to stop in Jerusalem and ponder what such ideas must have meant to Saul. The Antonia works to some degree, though it is long gone and we have only the Al-Omariya School for Boys, complete with Moslem minaret. The Roman ruins are helpful, too, especially newer excavations such as the Cardo that seem to slice downward through the city's layers to the Jerusalem of Saul. Yet for me, there are only two irreplaceable stops in the Pauline pilgrimage. For me, Saul's Jerusalem will always be a tale of two gates.

St. Stephen's Gate is the first required visit, in spite of its historical vagaries. It is tall, built of gray stone with battlements, and signed as though by an artist with two pairs of lions. This being Jerusalem, no one knows with certainty who put the lions there or what they symbolize; yet to this day many call it Lion's Gate. The main structure may have been built under Suleiman the Magnificent, and one story holds he saw the lions in a dream. Yet other tales hold that the lions may be older than even these Ottoman walls.

Tens of thousands of Christian pilgrims enter the Old City through this gate each Palm Sunday, recollecting with palms of their own the triumphal entry of Jesus into Jerusalem. The fact is, most now believe Jesus entered through what is called the Golden or Eastern Gate facing the Mount of Olives, and some maintain that it is from this gate that God's final trumpet will sound. This belief proved so persuasive to one Turkish governor in 1530 that he responded as best he could—by sealing off the gate! Nonetheless, there are those who believe the gate will be opened one final time, for Jesus to enter the holy city again. Today's pilgrims substitute St. Stephen's Gate, most processing from the Mount of Olives but some starting as far away as Bethany and ascending through Bethpage, bearing their palm fronds through the Garden of Gethsemane.

It is good to call up such images at St. Stephen's Gate, tangled as they are in fact and fantasy. Saul surely did not visit these places with the reverence we feel for them today. Most of his years in Jerusalem were spent before they had taken on such significance, though he may well have been in the city during the events themselves. The apostle Paul tells us nothing of such things in his letters—no actions or descriptions, no directional signals—reminding us implicitly that to him old Jerusalem was nothing but a city of Jews and later Christians; it was the new Jerusalem, the heavenly Jerusalem that mesmerized him, that called him always toward a future he knew would be dazzling.

That future first presents itself to Saul, and indeed history first presents Saul to us, at an event commemorated by St. Stephen's Gate. And what an understated presentation it is! "But he, filled with the Holy Spirit, looked up intently to heaven and saw the glory of God and Jesus standing at the right hand of God, and he said, 'Behold, I see the heavens opened and the Son of Man standing at the right hand of God.' But they cried out in a loud voice, covered their ears, and rushed upon him together. They threw him out of the city, and began to stone him. The witnesses laid down their cloaks at the feet of a young man named Saul'' (Acts 7:55-58).

Today, there are so many things we do not know about the martyrdom of St. Stephen, honored as the first Christian to die for his faith, beginning with where it really took place. Yet a remarkable amount of what we know about the faith for which he died, and about the dizzying vision in which

Scripture tells us he "fell asleep," comes to us from the Pharisee who stood off to the side, keeping an eye on the cloaks.

In time, or, as Paul might put it, "when the time had
fully come," the young man from Tarsus would cease standing at the side of human history, would instead take his place
with the One he came to see at its core. But that would re-
quire a revolution inside him, nothing less violent than the
insurrections that roused the Romans from the Antonia. It
is this interior coup d'etat that we recall at modern Jerusalem's most meaningful Pauline stop, returning in the morning sunlight.

Today's Damascus Gate, which even the 1967 renova-
tion could not completely rescue from Arab street venders,
ramshackle taxicabs, and its spidery skyline of TV antennas,
stands astride the two most important events in Paul's life.
We know quite a lot about this gate: how its existence goes
back to King Agrippa in the first century B.C., how the emperor Hadrian named it the Porta Neapolis because it led to
his "new city" on the ruins of biblical Shechem, how it was
rechristened St. Stephen's Gate in the fourth century by those
who placed the martyrdom nearby. It was Bab al Amad (an
Arabic name recalling a Roman pillar that supported a bust
of Hadrian), and finally, beginning in the seventeenth century, Damascus Gate. Above all, however, and indeed below all we see today, is the exit from Jerusalem taken by one
Jesus of Nazareth.

No palms, no kisses, no shouts of "Hosannah" accom-
panied him on this trip through the wall, out from the city
of life to the city of death. How many hours over the years
would Paul spend contemplating this single afternoon's agoniz-
ing journey, a journey he came to feel in his own blood and
bones and seek to feel all the more. And how many hours
would he spend turning before his eyes the most unlikely, con-
tradictory, and incredible aspect of that journey: it carried
Jesus, in truth and in history, from the city of death to the
city of life.

We sense this truth at the Damascus Gate, and we sense, too, the road that leads out from here, a straight shot north two hundred miles to the once-Roman, now-Syrian city that gives the gate its name. Saul passed this way, probably in the year 32, a Pharisee armed with God's Law and also with extradition papers for believers in the Way, followers of the now-disgraced Nazarene. Damascus was, for Saul, hardly the first such mission and not expected to be the last. Yet it was for all believers, and most of all for Saul, a journey that would change history.

The next time I would encounter his memory, not in Jerusalem but in a tiny, forgotten finger of southern Turkey, everything would be different. The believers would be calling themselves by a new name. And Saul himself, still ablaze with the zeal of the Pharisees, would be the very believer he had persecuted. He would be, perhaps above all, what he finally knew that Jewish law, Greek thought, and Roman vision could never make him: a free man.

Mt. Silpius Rising Above Antioch

4

ANTIOCH

Nations shall behold your vindication, and all kings your glory; You shall be called by a new name pronounced by the mouth of the Lord.

Isaiah 62:2

Then he went to Tarsus to look for Saul, and when he had found him he brought him to Antioch. For a whole year they met with the church and taught a large number of people, and it was in Antioch that the disciples were first called Christians.

Acts 11:25-26

The light that "apprehended" Saul on the road to Damascus, shining from the one he recognized as his Savior and asking the one question he least wanted to hear, "Why are you persecuting me?" has fascinated theologians, historians, and, yes, psychiatrists as long as the Christian story has been told. They ask many questions about this light, beginning with how real it was and ending with what it means to us today. Yet there is one question no one asks or feels the need to ask: How real was it to Saul? Every day of the rest of his life answered that question.

Though hardly a theologian, historian, or psychiatrist, I, too, have been fascinated by Saul's light as long as I can remember. Yet, even with its mysteries dazzling before me, I found nothing of its power in Tarsus or even in Jerusalem. For that matter, I did not feel called to seek it in Damascus, to identify Saul's spot on the road and wait there for some illumination to strike. That made no sense to me. The truth is, I felt my first awareness of this light in Antioch, among memories of the first community to call itself Christian. It was less a sighting than a sensing, less a presence than a promise. This must be, I thought, the way a blind man experiences the warmth of the sun.

It was a constant temptation to imagine Paul arriving in Antioch direct from Damascus, his heart bursting with the magnitude of God's good news, his arms reaching out to stop anyone who might listen as it cascaded from his lips. Antioch, even the shadow now known as Antakya in the Turkish province of Hatay, can inspire us to just such imaginings, as it tirelessly inspired me. Yet Scripture assures us such was not the case.

Paul preached first in the synagogues of Damascus, then went off alone to a place described as "Arabia." Later still, he traveled to Jerusalem for instruction (yet, he would insist, no form of commissioning) by those who had walked with Jesus. Finally, he spent a decade or more proclaiming his message of salvation to the people of Tarsus and Cilicia. Taken together, this virtually unchronicled period lasted fifteen to twenty years. It frustrates us no end to imagine the Paul we know from his letters missing so long from the Christian map. Yet it is only important that we remember, however little we know, that Paul saw himself at the center of every stage he mounted from the moment of his conversion until the moment of his death. He no doubt acted accordingly.

In Antioch, where Paul steps back into history's spotlight with no intention of stepping out, we are called to ponder the meaning of his conversion and the nature of the mission that grew from it with a passion unparalleled even among converts.

The event that changed the course of human history was, to Paul and to his avid chronicler in Acts, an exterior reality. In simple terms, it happened. The light truly did shine, and Jesus really did appear to Paul in the light. Yet even Paul shows time and again the interior component of this encounter: his vision of the Risen One was given, he says, not just "to me" but "in me." We are challenged to believe that in a single moment one man's systems of thought, feeling, and action were flooded with the tangible reality of God's love. Though Paul would spend a lifetime applying reason to this moment, on that road there was no reason. There was no argument. There was certainly no persuasive discourse. There was only the truth, revealed to him at the burning core of God's action. In this light, there was no past, only a present that demanded his all, and a future that cried out for transformation. Paul may have been blinded, yet from his light there was no turning away.

From the instant of his conversion, Paul experienced the intrusion of God into his life as immeasurably good news. Thus, he spoke of his personal revelation as "gospel" years before the narratives of Mark, Matthew, Luke, and John were set down. Many had preached of Jesus within his hearing, yet their words had driven him only to hatred and bloodshed. It was not talk of Jesus that transformed Paul, or even passion for Jesus: it was Jesus himself. When he speaks, in some translations, of being "apprehended by Christ Jesus" (Phil 3:12), Paul is expressing what we might call the interior violence that robbed him of one life and gifted him in the same moment with a dramatically different one.

The Paul we meet in Antioch never sees himself as one of the many who were preaching that Jesus was the Messiah promised to Israel, that he was crucified in atonement for sins, that he rose from the dead in victory over death and darkness. No, Paul could never be one of many. He sees himself, as recorded in Antioch onward, as a prime actor, a chosen instrument in God's long history of loving humankind. Thus when Acts has Barnabas bring Paul to Antioch and only then has Antioch call believers "Christians," we find ourselves pondering why this development carries Paul's fingerprints so tantalizingly.

Paul's mission—as Greek, as Roman, and as Jew—was to call the Gentile world into obedience to God's will in preparation for the ultimate salvation of Israel. Paul's mission, in Paul's eyes, was nothing less than God's mission. He carried Israel's salvation at the heart of his vision, preaching first nearly always in each city's synagogue. Yet the violent reaction of Jews to his proclamation, coupled with his certainty of a previously unrevealed Gentile role, made him realize that something larger than Judaism was at work. That something already possessed a new life; what it cried out for was a new name.

The Greek word that became that name in Antioch—Christianoi—shimmers before our eyes today. The more we understand its meanings, the more we are forced to think of Paul. We are told it may have started as an insult, applied to those who followed Jesus as Christ. Yet no one in history followed Jesus as Christ more fully than the Jew who became his voice among the people. We are told it may have been a recognition, given by Christians to each other as a sign of complete commitment. Yet no one in history displayed a commitment more complete than Paul's. Finally and most intriguingly, we are told it signified ownership, as when a slave was known only as an extension of his master. The link was so powerful at the time that some of our earliest records misspell Christos as Chrestos, a common name for slaves. However the Christians of Antioch came to understand their new name, it is certain Paul was at the center of their education, turning their eyes always to the master who had apprehended them from old bondage into his new and passionate service.

> *Now those who had been scattered by the persecution that arose because of Stephen went as far as Phoenicia, Cyprus and Antioch, preaching the word to no one but Jews. There were some Cypriots and Cyrenians among them, however, who came to Antioch and began to speak to the Greeks as well, proclaiming the Lord Jesus. The hand of the Lord was with them.*
>
> Acts 11:19-22

"Perhaps I could be of assistance to you in some way. . . ."

The words at first seemed part of a dream, for I had dozed off in the backseat of the taxi taking me away from the frenzy of Antioch's bus terminal. I had spent most of the morning bumping down along the Mediterranean, past the lonely ruins of Issos where Alexander had defeated Darius the Persian, between hazy blue mountains that curved inward or outward in thrust and parry with the sea. At last, when Antakya had seemed just beyond vision, we had climbed up onto an eruption of mountains and spent an hour snaking down their distant side.

The Arab-looking taxi driver would not take No for an answer, seeing through my empty insistence that I could walk just fine as far as I had to, with the heavy duffle bag over my shoulder. I finally surrendered, only to sense unspecified danger when he pulled to the side of a busy street, waved me into staying where I was, and stalked off up a shaded offshoot of the main artery. Obviously my sense of danger was real, but not real enough to keep me awake.

"Is there some way I can help you?"

My eyes finally focused on the face that seemed to fill the now-open taxi door. The face struck me as larger than life, though perhaps it was simply the shock of waking to see it there. It was all oversized, robust and ruddy, framed by generous white eyebrows and a carefully pointed white beard. I tried to smile, and thought of absolutely nothing to say.

"My friend, your taxi driver, said you looked lost. And as his English is not so good, he sought me out in case you needed help while here in Antakya. I have helped, you know, many who have come."

If at times before and after Antioch I seemed to be operating under a curse, Antioch was one huge blessing with one huge and impossibly lyrical name. The name was Husmamettin Altunay, belonging to the large man with the pencil-point beard, the gracious English, and the uncanny ability to be just around the corner whenever I needed help. When I had a question about the history of Antioch, I would step into a cafe and he would be there. When I felt confused about the meaning of anything Antiochene, I'd sit on a park bench and he would stroll by. When I would meet anyone in Antioch and struggle through a conversation, I learned without exception the person was on his way to meet a friend.

"Who is the friend you are meeting?" I came to ask with ever-increasing anticipation and delight.

"Husmamettin Altunay," was always the reply.

It was Altunay (who for more than two decades served as local director of the Turkish Ministry of Tourism) who started my mind on a trek into Antioch's surprising history. It was Altunay who pointed me toward the city's unforgettable Archaeology Museum, its rooms filled with Roman mosaics from the centuries before, during, and immediately after Paul. It was Altunay who talked me into staying at a hotel run by a friend of his, only to have the Atahan turn out to be a comfortable, impeccably run headquarters seemingly visited several times each day by anyone who matters in Antioch. And finally, it was Altunay, who with his successor at the local tourism office, gave me the least expected of gifts.

We were sitting in the ministry office that first afternoon, drinking tea and discussing my Pauline labor of love. Altunay had many suggestions, and before I left I would follow them all. Yet at that moment I was resisting their collective efforts at convincing me to rent a car. It sounds a bit silly now, disagreeing from a position of total ignorance with two bastions of local intelligence. But I had so convinced myself I could see Antioch on foot that I persisted beyond the point of any sane commitment.

"So," said the local director, a thin man introduced to me only as Mr. Kurt. He said nothing else in English, engaging instead in an extended flurry of Turkish—first with Altunay and then with someone at the other end of his telephone. Kurt set the phone back into the receiver, then flattened both his hands on his desk with a strange finality.

Roman Arch in Seleucia Peria

"The governor," he said, "gives his records."

I don't know what expression I wore upon hearing this short but enigmatic sentence. Yet I seemed to wear it for an eternity. My embarrassment was complete when Kurt felt compelled to repeat the message verbatim. "The governor gives his records."

I suppose, at that moment, my brain resembled some hi-tech wonder machine wrestling with a state secret intercepted in code. Key words flashed up again and again, along with possible combinations and meanings, all in a frenzy as I sat there sweating and speechless. Gives? Records? Offers . . . presents . . . delivers . . . turns over . . . records . . . recordings . . . sends. Sends! Records! Regards!

"Please tell the governor he is most kind," I blurted out, and the three of us smiled like children, happy the governor had sent his regards. We sent out for more tea.

"Here in this office," began Kurt, his expression giving away nothing, "we are very small and sadly we have no car." He glanced over at Altunay, then back to me. "The governor is sending his own car and driver for your use in the morning. They will be at your hotel at 9 o'clock, so you can please be ready at that time?"

That car and driver, along with the continuous rescues by Altunay in every corner of Antioch, threw open a door into the city's past that otherwise would have remained closed. Hour after hour, I moved through the streets and through the centuries, following what I hoped were the footprints of Paul. Even though they were seldom obvious, I was convinced there was no shortage of his footprints in Antioch.

The fact that at its height the city was outdone only by Rome and Alexandria is no mere happenstance. Antioch's importance, as it did so often in the ancient world, grew from its location. Seleucus I, a general under Alexander the Great, chose the site about 300 B.C. and named the city for either his father or his son, both of whom were called Antiochus. Antioch of Syria (as was its full name, among fifteen other Antiochs in Asia) lay twenty miles from the Mediterranean on the Orontes River. It spread out over the best land route between Asia Minor and Palestine, and boasted one of the principal harbors of the eastern Mediterranean where the Orontes flowed into the sea.

The Antioch known by Paul lay at the foot of Mt. Silpius, a 1660-foot peak over a plain three hundred feet above sea level. An island in the Orontes featured many of the most important buildings, including the palace, the racetrack, and the lovely colonnaded streets. The entire area, then as now, was cooled by a constant breeze off the Mediterranean funneled by mountains to Syria's desert sands. In the middle of summer, Antioch can feel like a crisp autumn day.

The city grew under the Seleucid kings until it attained both political importance and commercial prosperity. When Syria was annexed into the Roman empire in 64 B.C., Antioch was made capital of the new province and adorned by Julius Caesar, Augustus, and Tiberius, with considerable assistance from Herod the Great. Improved roads and expanded port facilities made for closer links with the Roman world, and closer links made for even more commerce. Pax Romana did its work well in Antioch.

As in Tarsus, Antioch at the time of Paul was a meeting place of Western and Eastern civilization. In the tangle of traditions that resulted, pagan cults that had boasted some consistency in the past faded into individual and diverse beliefs. The people of Antioch looked for God wherever they were in need, and fashioned God in whatever image made the most sense. Zeus and Apollo were joined here by all their brothers and sisters from the Pantheon, and also by Syrian cults devoted to Ba'al and a selection of mother goddesses. Mystery religions popular in that day promised an enticing mix of salvation and regeneration, but they offered little by way of theological system or social support.

Many Gentiles, therefore, found themselves drawn to precisely the place where system and support were cut from one cloth, the Jewish synagogue. Unlike those who surrendered to the superstition and immorality skewered with regularity by the Roman satirist Juvenal, those who entered into association with Judaism received an ethical system that could draw their actions into a semblance of meaning. And meaning, then as now, was a semblance of hope. The church, sect, or community of believers that inspired Barnabas to seek out Paul for service in Antioch was already enticingly "Pauline," with old barriers of race, nationality, and former religion fading into the background of something decidedly new.

The Antioch we can visit today includes all the surviving pieces from two thousand years that have not been particularly kind. Though a city of monumental importance in the early Church, the "Fair Crown of the Orient," with a population reaching 800,000, was badly damaged by an earthquake in 526 A.D., and reduced to rubble by a Persian siege in 540. The city as restored by the Emperor Justinian was again overrun in the seventh century, this time by Saracens who kept it in Moslem possession for more than three hundred years. Crusaders captured Antioch in 1098, leaving as their dramatic legacy a castle atop Mount Silpius; the sultan of Egypt wrestled the city from their hands less than two centuries later. It passed into Turkish control in 1516, remaining there until the end of World War I.

Nearly all we see spread before us in the Archaeology Museum was excavated from the city and from nearby Daphne during the period between this century's major wars. Between 1918 and 1938, what became known as the autonomous Sanjak of Iskenderun existed under French protection with its closest ties to Syria (which still claims the territory on many of its maps). In 1931 the Syrian government authorized Princeton University and the National Museum of France to excavate Antioch over a period of six years. Though there were many disappointments, the work was successful enough that it was allowed to continue a full two years beyond its official term. Hundreds of mosaic pavements, some depicting humans, animals, and plants, were discovered and removed intact.

Today's Antakya has only 80,000 inhabitants, many of whom seem more at home with memories of being a French protectorate than with being a part of the modern Turkish Republic. They exude a certain wistful air, one of resignation but not of bitterness. Not at all coincidentally, Antakya is one of the few Turkish cities with a significant number of Christians, who still draw great pleasure from living in the city chosen by God to give God's new people a name.

> *"It is too little, God says, for you to be my servant, to raise up the tribes of Jacob and restore the survivors of Israel; I will make you a light to the nations, that my salvation may reach to the ends of the earth."*
>
> Isaiah 49:6

It intrigued me throughout my days in Antioch that the local Christian community largely ignores the contribution of Paul, despite its confirmation in Scripture, in preference for an unconfirmable tradition involving Peter. According to this very early tradition, Peter came to Antioch to escape the persecutions in Jerusalem that, as we know from Acts, propelled the Church into its earliest expansion. I was told often that Peter founded the first Christian Church in history, right here in Antioch—a statement that, in reference to the word "Christian" seemed technically promising, but in reference to Peter seemed debatable.

Still, I didn't let my doubts keep me from visiting Antioch's single most famous Christian landmark. St. Peter's Church is a natural cave in the side of Mount Silpius in which the first of the new faith's services were believed to be held. The cave of gray and white stone, with its simple altar of much more recent construction, was for me a reminder of Paul's instruction by the Jerusalem "pillars" in the traditions of Jesus himself. This instruction gave him many prayers used by the young Church in celebrating a meal in their Savior's memory. Paul may well have preached on that meal, on its meaning, and on the mission to which it called those who partook of it, within these very walls.

On the final afternoon of my stay in Antioch, on the final advice of Husmamettin Altunay, I made my personal pilgrimage to the one place in the area indisputably associated with Paul. It was a bit of a trek, southwest to the city of Samandag, then along the coast a few miles north to a tumbledown fishing village called Cevlik. There were substantial ruins strewn about the highway leading into the village—Crusader and Ottoman—yet Altunay had directed me to a pair of rock outcroppings easily missed along the beach of dark sand. It thrilled me beyond expectation, as I stepped over these stones in the setting sun, to be standing atop the ancient breakwaters of Seleucia, the port from which Paul and Barnabas set sail on their first missionary journey.

This was no legend, no beloved tradition. This was Seleucia, whose marble Doric temple had for centuries signaled mariners that here was a deep-water port, fresh water, and the western terminus of an overland trade route streching from Antioch to the Far East. As I sensed in the impressive Roman ruins scattered over the surrounding hills, including a gargantuan tunnel built by the Emperor Titus, Seleucia was quite important in its day. Not only did it guard the mouth of the Orontes, it served as home port for the Roman fleet protecting the entire eastern Mediterranean.

Paul and Barnabas came to Seleucia in obedience to the Holy Spirit, searching for a ship that would help them fulfill the mission given them in Antioch. "Set apart for me Barnabas and Saul," the Spirit had said in prophecy, "for the work to which I have called them" (Acts 13:2). According to a later source, it took them three days to find a ship. They sailed by the outer breakwater under looming Mount Casios, then made for the open sea and Cyprus.

It was not what I knew of this missionary journey that excited me amid the stones of Seleucia, not the dramatic blinding of the magician at Paphos, not the confrontations with the Jews of Galatia. It was the sheer magnitude of what Paul and Barnabas were undertaking. I could not imagine what Barnabas must have thought as he watched their ship take on cargo; but I could, with effort and with Scripture, imagine something about Paul.

I tried to picture him here in Seleucia, a strategic port of the glorious and global Roman Empire. He may well have stood on this breakwater, as the light faded just as it was doing now, and pondered the sea with all its promise. He must have gazed out over this gentle surf to the calm of the dark deep waters. And he must, if only for an instant, have heard the entire earth crying out for deliverance. Years later, I wondered, could Paul have remembered the sound the world made during that sunset in Seleucia, as he described not just one empire but all of creation groaning as in labor, longing for the birth that had already begun, pleading for transformation? He must have remembered his own certainty on these stones, certainty that transformation was the very cargo he carried within the good news that filled his heart.

The Wilds of Paul's Galatia

5

GALATIA

The fruit of the spirit is love, joy, peace, kindness, generosity, faithfulness, gentleness, self-control. Against such there is no law.

Galatians 5:22-23

May I never boast except in the cross of our Lord Jesus Christ, through which the world has been crucified to me, and I to the world. For neither does circumcision mean anything, nor does uncircumcision, but only a new creation.

Galatians 6:14-15

After traveling a full day into the territory where Paul encountered the Galatians, and sleeping only fitfully at the shadowy Hotel Konya, I sat in the book-filled office of someone I gathered was either a lawyer or the owner of a car rental agency and waited for something to happen. I had already paid my ritual visit to Konya's tourism office, invested an hour downing tea with the director, and only then ascertained that no one there could help me. There was someone else, however, who might be able to help—a friend, he was called. So I found myself staring across a dark wooden desk at Ertugrul Ozdemir, listening as he spoke rapid Turkish in my direction, and wondering why there was a policeman in the office monitoring our every word.

The longer Ozdemir talked, in fact, the more uncomfortable I became. At first, an attractive young guide in blue jeans had joined us in the room; but then she excused herself saying she had never been to Pisidian Antioch, Derbe, or Lystra. It was clear enough she had never heard of them, and perhaps never heard of her own city by the name Paul used for it, Iconium. She whispered something about another commitment, shook my hand, and nervously made her exit.

Again I glanced over at the policeman, an exceedingly large, dark-haired man who appeared ready to burst from his pale green shirt and dark green pants. He was wearing a revolver that seemed equally large, perhaps catching my eye more regularly than I wish it had. He broke into all the Turkish, finally, with adept and British-accented English.

"Perhaps," he said, "you are wondering why I am here. . . ."

The presence of the policeman, it turned out, was only the first of many things I would wonder about as I struggled through the land known to us from the overlay of Paul's incendiary Letter to the Galatians and the narrative in Acts of the Apostles. The questions about this chapter in his mission cut as deeply as questions can: Who were Paul's Galatians? Where was Paul's Galatia? Where, in our day, are the ruins of Paul's Galatian cities? Later in my journey, I would confront mysteries more dazzling and perhaps more complex; yet never would I confront as many mysteries, one atop the other, with as many open and empty miles of crumbling country road in between.

I was searching for the places Paul had preached to the people he called Galatians. I had the record in Acts, from his first and second missionary journeys, and of course I had his letter. But if, as Acts assures us, "the word of the Lord spread throughout the region," my own attempts to cover the same ground would flow neither naturally nor without trepidation. It seemed that Ozdemir knew where these places were. It seemed he had a car and was going to take me to some or all of them. It seemed the policeman was going to accompany us. Everything seemed. Nothing was certain. And places with names only far-off scholars knew were waiting for us somewhere in the dust.

Suddenly everyone in the office stood up and started for the door: Ozdemir, the policeman, and the man from the local tourism office. I rose, too, only to be halted abruptly. Ozdemir tapped his forehead, as though to say "How silly of me!", and pushed back through us to a file cabinet in the corner. From it he extracted a glistening military .45 pistol, assured himself it was loaded, then stuffed it into his belt.

"Okay," he said, shifting into the only English he would use all day. "Now we may go."

> *But when the fullness of time had come, God sent his Son, born of a woman, born under the law, to ransom those under the law, so that we might receive adoption. As proof that you are children, God sent the spirit of the Son into our hearts, crying out, "Abba, Father!" So you are no longer a slave but a child, and if a child then also an heir, through God.*
> Galatians 4:4-7

As we bounced across the plain toward Yalvac, where the map promised ruins of Pisidian Antioch, I didn't know whether to feel well-protected or in the gravest danger. I knew that two of the four people in the car were armed, and I couldn't rule out a gun somewhere on the third. Yet I realized, as we crossed countryside more vacant than any I had ever seen, that my intimations of something sinister ran deeper than any fear of being shot.

This was a wild, unpredictable, even dangerous place, this plain of billowing yellow grass as thick as an animal's winter fur. Except for angry outcroppings of lunar rock, I could see as far as my eyes were capable, with nothing even tempted to get in the way. There seemed to be no villages, though the occasional plot of land appeared to be farmed, and no truckloads of workers heading into or out of the fields. There was only this plain, and it was hard to imagine Paul wishing to spend much time here.

In a flash, as we bumped our way west at much too high a speed, I caught sight of a single bent-over man leading a brown bear along the highway—a sullen performer at peasant markets, no doubt, as lonely and lost as Paul must sometimes have imagined himself. This land cut him off from all he knew. Most of all, I thought suddenly, it cut him off from the sea. The Mediterranean seemed a universe removed from this somber interior landscape, the sea with its sunlight and promise and possibility of escape. For all the open expanse of this territory, there was also a sense of being trapped. I could not imagine Paul wanting just to get in and get out, to do his job and make a run for the coast. Yet that was precisely what I wanted to do.

All the same, the dreary drive from Konya had given me time to consolidate all I knew about Galatia and about the people Paul once branded "stupid Galatians." The fact is, I had been troubled reading his Galatian letter, and it was an unease I could not shake. Even with its serenades to the saving faith of Abraham, the letter struck me as bitter and hateful about Jews. At its worst, in its attacks on those who wished to "Judaize" early Christianity, it seemed bitter and hateful about being Jewish. I longed for understanding. The drive had given me time to distill from a memory of books and battered maps all I needed to learn.

Today, the reality of this journey forces us to choose between cities annihilated by failure and cities obliterated by success. Iconium is certainly of the second type, since modern Konya seldom pauses to remember its past as a Roman market center. Pisidian Antioch has no memory for quite the opposite reason, having no one around to remember. And in the cases of Derbe and Lystra, all traces of their habitation have been so covered over that even experts argue over their location. A stone here, an inscription there, a drawing in an out-of-print book—I was working with far less than the experts. Yet here I was, trying to kick over the same soil, to

Lystra's Mound Across a Field
of Flowers

breathe the same air as the Galatians who heard and read of Jesus from Paul.

As a region, Galatia was only one of many Roman provinces in the first century A.D., taking its place with Achaia, Macedonia, Bithynia, and a host of others strewn about the world of the Caesars. It took its name from the Celtic people who came to be known first as Gauls and later as Galatians, setting their stamp on a mix of peoples living almost as far north as the Black Sea and almost as far south as the Mediterranean. Galatia meandered more than four hundred miles, forming a huge "S" through what was then Asia Minor. Three cities in the northern section—Ancyra (now the capital of Turkey, Ankara), Tavium, and Pessinus—were inhabited by the fiercely independent Celts, while the cities to the south became more cosmopolitan.

It fascinated me to note that while I found not one population in my south Galatia, Paul found four in his. There were the usual Greeks and Romans, hanging onto empires lost and empires found. There were remnants of the earlier Phrygian civilization that had first tried to wrestle this land under control. And there was a solid Jewish community that had prospered in the region's quartet of cities since the days of Seleucid rule. As recorded in Acts, this tangle of traditions extracted from Paul one of the longest sermons attributed to any apostle (Acts 13:16-41), given in the synagogue of Pisidian Antioch and exhorting Jews to embrace Jesus as their long awaited Messiah.

Nothing of the synagogue remains today. In fact, virtually nothing of the city itself has survived the incessant beatings of earthquake and invasion. Yet we do have an extended stretch of aqueduct nearby, a weathered-stone gray-brown snake in the shadow of mountains that would be at home on the moon. And we do know that, contrary to the surviving evidence, Pisidian Antioch was the region's most important city and the site of Paul's earliest efforts as a missionary to a major population center.

There can be no doubt that this Antioch visited by Paul and Barnabas was a fine city built on a plateau high above the Anthius River. There were at least two magnificent public squares, with an impressive stairway leading from one to the other. The Pisidian city was viewed in its day as a miniature Rome in the hinterland of Asia.

In his synagogue address, Paul set the saving act of Jesus within the long history of Israel, one of human suffering and infidelity marked by the promise and constancy of God. The death and resurrection of Jesus, he said, marked the fulfillment of lifetimes of longing, the light for generations who had lived in darkness. "We ourselves," said Paul, "are proclaiming this good news to you that what God promised our ancestors has been brought to fulfillment for us" (Acts 13:32-33). Yet as a sad prophecy for all his Galatian work, Paul drew upon Israel's own prophets to warn against hearing this news and walking away unchanged. "Look on, you scoffers, be amazed and disappear. For I am doing a work in your days, a work that you will never believe even if someone tells you" (Acts 13:41).

On the following sabbath, the entire city of Antioch gathered to hear Paul and Barnabas. Noting that the crowds were filled with Gentiles, the Jews who apparently had been impressed initially now contradicted the apostles with violent abuse. Angrily, they pointed out these very Gentiles belonged to a pagan cult whose chief god was Men, and that some had even begun worshipping the Roman emperor. Unshaken by these charges, Paul and Barnabas began to preach of Jesus among the Gentiles.

Driven by the Jews from Pisidian Antioch yet "filled with joy and the Holy Spirit" (Acts 13:52), the apostles headed southeast to Iconium. Though Paul and Barnabas exited Antioch with their often-quoted "We now turn to the Gentiles," they showed what that did not mean by beginning again in the synagogue. As the crowds in Iconium duplicated the hysteria of Pisidia, they pushed on quickly to Derbe and Lystra.

The Path Leading to "New" City
of Ilystra

At the eastern extreme of my day's long and loping circle through Paul's Galatia, Derbe waited in a conspiracy of silence. To this day, its exact location is uncertain, though the evidence for the site at Kerti Huyuk turned persuasive in 1962. Before that, there was no agreement; most of the scholarly opinion favored a different site altogether. All we know about ancient Derbe comes from The Acts of the Apostles. That, it turns out, is little indeed.

Paul's visits must have produced no major oral traditions, for we know only that he preached in Derbe during his first and second missionary journeys (Acts 14:20 and 16:1), and possibly again during his third (Acts 18:23). One final Scripture reference concerns Gaius, Paul's disciple from Derbe, who joined him for the trip from Corinth to Macedonia and Asia (Acts 20:4).

The district known in ancient times as Galactic Lycaonia, which included Iconium, Derbe, and Lystra, is bounded on the south by the Taurus Mountains and Paul's native Cilicia, on the north by the often-eerie Cappadocian hills. Huge empty expanse follows huge empty expanse between the rises that define Lycaonia's limits, making it difficult to choose one patch of ground over another and declare "This was Derbe." And the handful of non-Scriptural allusions that we possess are no more detailed than the mentions in Acts of the Apostles.

Alexander the Great seems to have brought Greek culture to Derbe, though it is unclear how much of it took hold. Later, a chieftain with the name Antipater caught the attention of Strabo. Antipater, called a "brigand" and "pirate" by the historian, used Derbe as his residence until the emperor Augustus allowed another local king to kill him and take his lands. When that king died, a quarter century before the birth of Jesus, the territory passed into Roman control. Derbe itself spent several decades as part of the province of Galatia, then, under Augustus, entered a period of rule by princes handpicked by the emperor. Moving into Paul's day, the city was attached to the Cilician kingdom of Antiochus IV. It even took on the prefix Claudia for a time, in honor of the emperor Claudius.

As late as 1877, scholars were trying to locate Derbe, based on the location of Lystra. With Lystra presenting mysteries of its own, Derbe was a virtual impossibility. Seven years later, J.R. Sitlington Sterrett identified the ruins of Lystra near Katyn Serai, twenty-two miles southwest of Iconium, then proceeded to place Derbe near the large mound of Gudelisin. Despite considerable bickering, the Gudelisin location was promoted by the persuasive W. M. Ramsay in his 1908 book, *The Cities of St. Paul*. Yet even Ramsay acknowledged the ruins were so extensive in the area that Derbe may have occupied more than one site, with what he called "sepulchral monuments" lining the road between them. H. V. Morton's 1937 book, *In the Steps of St. Paul*, tells of his failure to identify Derbe, even after extensive driving across primitive trails of the plain.

The site I visited burst into prominence in the middle of this century, with the publication of an inscription found in 1956 in Kerti Huyuk, thirty miles east of the Derbe proposed by Sterrett and Ramsay. The sixteen-line inscription, apparently made in 157 A.D., may be partially translated "the gods of Derbe having manifested themselves, the council and people, in the time of Cornelius Dexter, the governor dedicated this altar." A second inscription uncovered in 1962 supports this initial piece of limestone evidence, pointing again to the mound of Kerti Huyuk and describing one Bishop Michael of Derbe as a "most God-loving person."

Today the windswept mound is strewn with pottery dating back to the Iron Age as well as the Greek and Roman periods. All we can sense of this lost city is that Derbe was significant, enough so that some of its inhabitants could afford imported ceramic ware. Otherwise, we have only another nameless place on the plain. I caught myself remembering the matter-of-fact report in Acts: Paul and Barnabas "proclaimed the good news to that city and made a considerable number of disciples" (Acts 14:21). It alarmed me, to no small degree, that such dramatic events could seem so mundane at a distance of two thousand years.

We reached Lystra in the late afternoon, and my disappointment was almost disabling. Yet another day of my journey had passed, turning up an aqueduct, a mound, and now another mound. The brown-green mass rising above a field of yellow flowers returned my blank stare, assuring me that Paul's Lystra, like the heart of his letter to these stubborn Galatians, would remain just beyond my grasp.

What I sensed was an element of the primitive, the pagan, that even great, enlightening forces could not overcome. Lystra, like Derbe and the rest of the region, had been Greek and Roman; it had seen the work of ambitious human hands building and shaping this larger world. Yet it had remained a captive of its fear, viewing heaven as a place more of wrath than of abiding love. In one of Lystra's most persistent legends, the gods Zeus and Hermes had come to earth as humans and found so little welcome that they destroyed the entire population. When Paul and Barnabas healed a crippled man, the people of Lystra were determined not to make this mistake again. They declared the apostles Hermes and Zeus and prepared to sacrifice animals in their honor (Acts 14:13).

Paul and Barnabas are credited by Scripture with a tiny gem of a response, outlining how God had worked from age to age even among the Gentiles. "God was not without witness," they declared, "for God gave you rains from heaven and fruitful seasons, and filled you with nourishment and gladness for your hearts" (Acts 14:17). Yet even these words were not enough to quell the disturbance. It took Jews from Pisidian Antioch and Iconium to accomplish that, turning the Lystrans with frightening speed from deification to hatred and fear. The same people who had proclaimed Paul a god now pelted him with stones, dragged him from the city and left him only when they thought he was dead.

Somewhere in or behind this story, I decided, lurked that something sinister I had felt all day as we made our way across the Galatian plain. Yet any effort to search this mound until I found it was cut short by my compatriots shouting at me from across the field of flowers.

"It is late," Ozdemir explained when I had returned to the car, the policeman serving as translator. "This is nothing here, this Lystra. There is one more place you must see before there is no light."

It was too late and we were on our way by the time I realized I didn't want to see another place. I wanted to stalk up and down the sides of Zordula Huyuk, shaking from my heart all confusion and disappointment, trying to move forward. I wanted to find my own spot against the dirt and stones and read Paul's Galatian letter from greeting to farewell, listening for whatever it might say to me. I wanted to understand. Instead, I had only this car full of armed men, each apparently convinced that all I really needed lay somewhere at the end of yet another road.

> *Through the law I died to the law, that I might live for God. I have been crucified with Christ; yet I live, no longer I, but Christ lives in me; insofar as I now live in the flesh, I live by faith in the Son of God who has loved me and given himself up for me.*
>
> Galatians 2:19-21

A strange anxiety overtook me by the time Ozdemir parked the car at the bottom of a curving, rock-strewn road that led up around a gray cliff face. It would be dark soon, with no light left to revisit Lystra, no matter how much I begged or tried to bully. Besides, they had all the weapons. In the last instant before shutting my door and hearing it lock automatically, I bent back in and grabbed my Bible. With it tucked under my arm, I sprinted up the road to join my companions.

They were talking, all three in Turkish and all three at a level of excitement I had not heard all day. They did not stop when I pulled in alongside. I concentrated instead on the way the road grew steeper as it twisted painfully against the cliff, with a ragged wall of stones between us and a drop to the plain far below. My soft shoes proved unequal to the climbing, my feet bending around each smooth stone and crying out at each sharp one.

The policeman's English caught me by surprise. "You see, our friend says this place is not on any map. And the tourism ministry does not even know about it." The man from the tourist office shrugged and smiled, offering what confirmation he could. Then the policeman continued as we climbed. "This place is not known, and not recognized. It is why I came with you today, to help you understand. Our friend wanted you to see it, because he feels there is something here for you."

Ozdemir halted, so we gathered around him. He ran his hand through the air along the path we had just climbed, then up past us and between a pair of huge boulders on either side of the path. He spoke rapidly as he gestured, stopping after every few sentences to let the policeman translate.

"Many people do not know of this place," he said. "Certainly not the tourism ministry. At the university in Konya, they know something of it, but there are no resources to learn more. Turkey is a poor country. It is hard to think of archaeology when there is need of food, of water, of electrical power. But I have read many books, and I have studied many ancient coins. What I know about this place, I know for the most part from coins. This place is known as Ilystra. It is very mysterious and very old, perhaps as old as your St. Paul."

With a brief smile, Ozdemir motioned for us to follow him. We passed through the boulders, which I suddenly knew to be gates, and climbed onto the back of a mountain that had nearly two thousand years ago supported a shimmering city above the plain. The wind roared across the flat sections of rock, ripping in at us through mountain passes we could see in the hazy distance.

"Just over there," said Ozdemir, "is the little village of Gokyurt." I made him write the name on my map so I would remember it. "And over there, perhaps fifteen kilometers, is the Lystra we visited. Lystra is older, we know that. Ilystra is younger, we know that. What we don't know is what happened, and when, and why. Something happened, though, probably in the first century. Perhaps an earthquake, or some terrible disease. And the people of Lystra traveled along the road we see far below us, up the path through the gates we just climbed, to where we are now. Perhaps in ancient days both cities existed together, maybe for a long time. But at one point the old city simply died, and this city on this mountain found new life."

I was stunned, as though a photograph long before my eyes shifted suddenly into focus. Standing at the center of what was Ilystra, gazing far down at the road to Lystra, I realized I was also standing at the center of Paul's Galatian letter. In its pages, I realized, Paul instructs, reminds, encourages, rages, and pleads, all that we embrace a single truth. Gentile or Jew, it does not matter, he says. Both are shackled to an incomplete vision of God's past, and both cling to it in fear, even in the dazzling light of God's future. Paul asks Gentile and Jew the same question: how can you slink back to your old, abandoned city of death when Christ Jesus has built for you a glistening new city of life?

"Come quickly!" the policeman shouted. "Come now! Please! Our friend says you must see!"

Sprinting across an open stretch of crumbled stone, I joined Ozdemir, the policeman, and the man from the ministry at the edge of a cliff. With them, I stared down silently at a shape just out of reach and nearly hidden among the rocks. It was an ancient church, carved from the same gray rock that formed city and mountain and plain. It was tiny, and it seemed even tinier from above. I shivered involuntarily. The church was built in the shape of a cross.

Amid the Thorns Atop Colossae

6

COLOSSAE

I say this that no one may deceive you by specious arguments. For even if I am absent in the flesh, yet I am with you in spirit, rejoicing as I observe your good order and the firmness of your faith in Christ.

Colossians 2:4-5

It is Christ in you, the hope for glory. It is he whom we proclaim, admonishing everyone and teaching everyone with all wisdom, that we may present everyone perfect in Christ.

Colossians 1:27-28

I stepped out onto the second-floor balcony of my small and otherwise empty hotel on the highway between Denizli and Pammukale, trying to see whether Nur and our driver had arrived. Even in the chalk-white mist that obscured the highway and much of the hotel entrance, I could see that my search for Colossae was not quite ready to begin.

I had found Nur in Denizli the afternoon before and with her help had arranged to keep a taxi as long as it took to find Colossae. She assured me as a local guide that she knew where it was, pointing earnestly at the village called Honaz on my map, even though she had never had reason to visit it. The taxi driver insisted he knew, then conceded it would be his first visit as well. After all, he asked through Nur's translation, why would anyone wish to go there? He had grown up in this area and had never met anyone who had been to Colossae.

I smiled as I leaned against the cold steel of the balcony, remembering. The name Nur, she'd explained, is Turkish for "Light." Okay, I had thought, I've found you. Let's see if I can find Colossae.

A sharp but none-too-insistent horn cut through the mist and I circled down the steel staircase, then cut across the wet grass to the highway. Nur greeted me at the hotel gate, and our driver waved with the arm that was resting on his window. Both seemed more serious than they had the evening before, when we had been joined by Nur's husband of only a month for the one indispensable tourist activity Pammukale has to offer.

With our shoes and socks in hand and our pants legs rolled up, we had marched like some diminutive bus tour through the bizarre mineral waterfalls forming white terraces along a steep and eerie mountainside. Strangely, some of the mirror-like pools were too hot to enter, while others felt almost frozen. Yet all the springs came forth from the same mountain, and hot existed side by side with cold. The terraces, Nur explained, had been here in Paul's day, though not nearly so vast without the intervening two thousand years of formation. The springs had certainly been here, she said, capturing the interest of all ancient civilizations who had chosen to live in this place.

We had played in the pools until dark, taking turns snapping each other's photographs. For Nur and her husband, I gathered, this was part of a honeymoon they would enjoy only in pieces strewn about the early years of their marriage. But now things were different. Nur's husband was off doing his job, and she was doing hers. And we had to find a city that had existed two millennia earlier—had lived and breathed and faltered—and then had disappeared in this mist.

We had one initial stop to make: the region's best-developed ancient site, Hierapolis. This was the city that grew up around the bounty of these mineral springs. It finds the briefest of mentions in the Letter to the Colossians, as one of the cities in the ministry of Paul's associate Epaphras.

The ruins are extensive enough to warrant government fences, including the seats of a theater and the remains of several churches. One church, in fact, is named for St. Philip, ostensibly "the evangelist" in The Acts of the Apostles (21:8-9). A tradition at least as interesting concerns Philip's quartet of daughters. According to Eusebius in the fourth century, three of these remained unmarried and died in Hierapolis. The fourth took a husband and "lived in the Holy Spirit," being buried to the west, in Ephesus.

The cemetery gives ample evidence of wealth in Hierapolis. Many of the tombs bear inscriptions that cast light on social status, and on religious affiliation as well. The lid of one sarcophagus carries a seven-branched menorah and some poorly carved Greek characters that can be translated, "Belonging to the Jews."

Anxious as I was to reach Colossae, or at least to deal with the problems I had by this time learned to expect, I waved Nur away from the small Hierapolis museum. "It is very fine," she told me, "with many antiquities of note." I promised to visit another time, when I could do them justice, and motioned her toward the car. Yet even my anxiety was stopped in its tracks by a rusting, half-fallen sign I spotted almost as soon as we were speeding along the highway.

"Nur," I said, with hesitation, "that sign said something like 'Laodicea.' Isn't that some place famous, the city in the Bible?"

"Certainly," she replied. "Lao-dikia," she repeated, substituting the hard "k" for my soft "c."

"Is there anything still there? To see? I mean, can we go there?"

"I do not know. I have never been. And no one mentioned it in guide's school." She stopped, apparently hoping Laodicea's absence from her guide school's curriculum would dissuade me. She was visibly confused, wondering why anyone would rush off without visiting the Hierapolis museum, and then ask to spend who-knows-how-much time in the middle of nowhere. What was to be done? she asked herself. To me she said only, "As you wish."

After a brief exchange in Turkish, our driver stopped the car in the center of the highway, then backed nearly a mile at high speed to the sign that, yes, still promised "Laodicea." For an uncomfortable moment, I thought perhaps I'd imagined it. The driver nodded in the direction of the sign, clearly troubled by the dirt road rutted by farmers' carts that led off through mist and high grass. I waved my hand toward the grass but he still didn't believe me. Nur assured him this was really what their strange and difficult passenger had in mind.

The road led upward through the grass, tilting continuously from one side to the other. It straightened out just long enough to pass through a tiny village, then returned to its former ways. At times the ruts were so deep the car had to excavate their central peak. There was much grinding of gears.

At last we came up over the top of the hill, parked the car at the end of the trail, and walked through the ruins of Laodicea. They seemed almost lost among the grass and thorns, huge green-brown stones rising from nothing to form an archway here, a crumbled pile there. As close as we could tell, the ruins were minimal: pieces of a theater, a stadium, a bath, and what seemed to be a water tower. Yet the view, even sifted through the rolling mist, was magnificent. Mountains to the east seemed to stumble as they neared Laodicea, falling flat when they reached the Lycus River and the valley that stretched west as far as Ephesus.

"Laodicea," Nur said haltingly, "is mentioned in your Bible, in the book of your St. John of Patmos." Somewhere in her life, Nur had learned this book's author and its traditional place of composition, an island off the Turkish coast. Yet she had not quite committed to memory the name by which it is commonly known: Revelation. "There was no cold water here," she continued. "And any hot water had to come all the way from Hierapolis, in these ceramic pipes you see through the limestone. By the time it reached Laodicea, it was not hot anymore."

She stopped and smiled, proud of her little story about water temperature. At first I did not understand, which made her smile all the more.

"Remember your St. John," she teased.

I remembered. Fumbling through the pages of my Bible, I finally found the place and read just loud enough for Nur to hear. "To the angel of the church in Laodicea, write this: The Amen, the faithful and true witness, the source of God's creation, says this: I know your works; I know that you are neither cold nor hot. I wish you were either cold or hot. So, because you are lukewarm, neither hot nor cold, I will spit you out of my mouth. For you say, 'I am rich and affluent and have no need of anything,' and yet do not realize that you are wretched, pitiable, poor, blind and naked" (Rev 3:14-17).

A chilly wind blew deep furrows across the grass, even as the sun burned off the mist. It was time to make our way to Colossae.

For in him were created all things on heaven and earth, the visible and the invisible, whether thrones or dominions or principalities or powers; all things were created through him and for him. He is before all things, and in him all things hold together.

Colossians 1:16-17

Though we know the Lycus Valley primarily for the mysterious "heresy" that inspired Paul to write his letter on placing trust in Christ, in the apostle's day it was famous throughout the Roman world for its trio of prominent cities. Colossae takes scriptural pride of place, yet both Hierapolis and Laodicea have roles in the evangelization of Asia Minor that are reflected in both Acts and Paul's epistles. While Paul directed these efforts from Ephesus during his extended ministry there, he was assisted by a number of followers in the Lycus Valley itself. Most believe the Churches in Colossae, Hierapolis, and Laodicea were planted by Paul's "fellow slave" Epaphras, whose report on the progress of that first city would one day set Paul to writing (Col 1:7).

Centuries before the work of Paul and Epaphras, however, the dark and compelling mysteries of Colossian belief were taking root on the banks of this chalky river. The city no doubt existed before the sixth century B.C., and it was considered "great" by the time of Herodotus, whose history describes the march of the Persian King Xerxes in 481 B.C. Cyrus the Younger also passed through Colossae, this time in 401, as described by Xenophon. A large population and the city's presence on a trade route between Ephesus and Syria kept the people of Colossae current, ready to debate and in many cases embrace the latest styles of thinking.

The single greatest controversy in the city's pre-Christian history is a foreshadowing of the errors that so troubled Paul. As far back as Herodotus, it was believed that the Lycus flowed underground for two miles before emerging near Colossae. The later geographer Strabo also noted this underground passage, a mysterious journey that ended at the Meander and Cadmus rivers closer to Ephesus. As the river now flows beside the city, scholars over the centuries have struggled to substantiate these early descriptions. Yet most of what they have found is the darkest of myths.

A legend predating written history tells of a great flood that threatened Colossae with destruction. Elemental forces in the universe intervened, opening a rock so that the river could flow through. Clearly, this legend was an attempt to explain the massive gorge near Colossae through which the river flowed; the "underground" element was confusion caused by the sight of water below and rocks high above. Yet even an early Christian effort to attach this legend to the archangel Michael could not obscure the presence here of a deep and lasting superstition. The people of the Lycus were so fearful of spirits they would one day question the liberating power of Paul's gospel message.

The second element in the Colossian error arrived in the city some two centuries before the birth of Jesus. The historian Josephus weaves into our tapestry the arrival of Babylonian Jews—followers of a Judaistic variant grounded less in Scripture than in ritual baths and ceremonies built around wine. As these Jews settled in the Lycus Valley, the same vulnerability to cultural pressures described in the Babylonian Talmud made them ripe for the area's ancient subservience to unseen powers. The false teaching of Paul's day, then, found rich soil in the two major theological strands of Colossae's past.

These errors also found support in the volatile physical world that residents of the valley knew all too well. In addition to the gorge considered a subterranean passage created by angels, there were hundreds of sulphur springs that emitted odors as though from a hidden and evil kingdom below. And there were frequent tremors and minor earthquakes, each a reminder to the Colossians of battles fought just beyond their sight. Angel worship became the single most prominent form of religion in Colossae. Coming into the apostolic period, the city was a spawning ground for any number of mysterious cults, and a living pulpit for any number of wild prophets.

We are tempted to make too much, perhaps, of Colossae's dark and unrecorded ending, a fitting final chapter to all that went before. According to the Roman historian Tacitus, the city may have been destroyed by an earthquake in the first century A.D. If so, it was rebuilt in some form, for the Christian Church there remained active for several centuries. One bishop from Colossae signed a decree at a council in 692; another appeared at the seventh general council at Nicaea in 787. Eventually, Colossae was simply abandoned, surrendered to the white mists that rise from the chalk-impregnated stream that once was a powerful river. The Lycus had been powerful enough, in fact, to have shifted even Christianity from its proper course.

Before we seek more precise understanding of Paul's letter, it is essential that we grasp two sides of the same theological coin. First, despite the occasional use of the word "heresy" in relation to these efforts, the elements that make a belief truly heretical did not yet exist. Neither the established doctrine from which to depart nor the defiance that makes such departures dangerous were part of Church life at the time. Scripture assures us the expansion of Christianity was both mandated by Jesus and directed by the Spirit that descended at Pentecost. Yet we see little evidence that all teachers proclaimed God's good news with precisely the same elements or emphasis.

With his often unparalleled insight into Christ's saving act, Paul saw clearly when men and women embarked on roads that diluted, undercut, or threatened the meaning of that act in their lives. And he sought, with love if also with frustration, to turn them back onto the right road.

It is intriguing to recognize in the Colossian controversy the two most virulent problems faced by the Church in its first century of life. As in Galatia, we see in Colossae the strange and, to Paul, potentially lethal work of early Christianity's "Judaizers." We see their efforts to construct a Christianity not on Jewish foundations but of carelessly chosen Jewish bricks. The preachers of Colossae sought to call believers into a tangle of practices and prohibitions aimed at appeasing an angry and crowded heaven. Even so, the ascetic practices in Colossae required a different style of confrontation by Paul than they had in Galatia, precisely because of their second element.

In the Colossian letter, we see one of the Church's earliest assaults on a style of relating to God that later would be termed "gnosticism." Rooted in the Greek word "gnosis" (knowledge), this was a system of beliefs—indeed any system of beliefs—that proclaimed its adherents an intellectual or spiritual elite gifted by God with a vision God had withheld from others. Invariably, following a path clearly marked by Gentile pagans and by such Jewish sects as the Essenes, gnosti-

Farmer's View of Mound
at Colossae

cism emphasized initiation into a select circle and growth along a road to a perfect knowledge of God. Many elements of gnosticism fit comfortably into Jewish belief, particularly the emphasis on one group's place in God's history and its adherence to legal regulations in every aspect of its life. In Colossae, gnosticism by its own measurement seemed to fit comfortably into Christian belief until Paul wrote his letter.

Because Paul's responsibility is to the Colossians (and not primarily to us), he feels no need to describe in detail the beliefs he is calling into question. These we have reconstructed over the centuries, both from Paul's side of the "conversation" and from earlier Jewish and pagan practices. In the name of the Christian Church, the Colossians had been seduced into adopting a world view in which both the delivery and enforcement of God's law were functions of angelic powers that ruled the universe. Breaking the law set people in bondage to these angels, these lords of the elements; and only the strictest adherence to ascetic practices could bring about deliverance.

The angels, in the Colossian view, patrolled the lines of communication between God and the people, with only worship that passed their censorship being allowed. Their mediation was complete, forcing even Jesus to submit to their will on his way to earth and back again. These were angels who were more than angels, more than shimmering messengers of God's work and word as seen throughout Jewish and Christian Scripture. These were spiritual rulers with kingdoms of their own, possessed of dizzying autonomy. These were, as Paul would argue, principalities and powers.

The Colossian error seems a marvel of theological engineering, admirable in its complexity and seductive in its potential. Yet Paul's response was, in essence, so simple that it must have caught many Colossians by surprise. Others surely were angered by it, depriving them as it did of fears on which they had learned to depend. And still others, sensing its promise, must have felt themselves set free, lifted from the very chains they had constructed from their own fears.

As for me, over the years, reading Paul's Letter to the Colossians had produced only doubt and confusion—until I read it once more atop the mound at Colossae.

> *So as you received Christ Jesus the Lord, walk in him, rooted in him and built upon him and established in the faith as you were taught, abounding in thanksgiving.*
>
> Colossians 3:10-11

It is presumed from his letter that Paul never visited Colossae, a logical extension of his reference to "you and to those in Laodicea and all who have not seen me face to face" (Col 2:1). For a time, it seemed, I was not to visit Colossae either, considering the controversies we had in our own car over just where this place might be. The driver took us to his notion first; he was the driver, after all. Yet where he took us there was nothing. Then Nur had her turn, leading us along a series of roads that ended in nothing as well. At this point, awkward as it made me feel between two locals, I suggested we try where I thought Colossae was.

My theory was based neither on superior map-reading skills nor on any enhanced sense of direction. It was built on a single moment I'd experienced as we drove, when suddenly all the fields and trees and rocks had rushed into momentary focus, a focus I remembered from somewhere. The vision was one I had seen, no doubt in one of the countless out-of-print books I had perused before beginning my journey. We had driven, in that split-second, through some old photograph of Colossae, and I insisted we go back and check the picture more closely.

We turned off the main road onto a simple mud track. Yet within one hundred feet of climbing, we noticed that the sides of the path were littered with bits of gracefully sculpted marble, as though they were so much waste paper. Even the walls between fields, ostensibly constructed of piled stones, were studded with ancient faces, animals, and inscriptions. There was in all this the eerie sensation of visiting a grave-yard, one whose headstones were formed of old bones.

Our driver pulled to a stop and climbed out to a gather-ing of peasant women taking a break from their work. This became an extremely loud and animated conversation, with many hands pointing in many directions, until a young man seemed to appear from the midst of the women's colorful silks. He spoke a few short sentences to our driver, who then turned and beckoned us to follow.

"Colossae," he said.

Our driver stayed behind, probably with the intention of taking a nap in the car. Nur and I followed the young man. He had apparently picked up some education, for he alone seemed to understand the significance of the white marble re-mains his ancestors had used to shore up their roads and build their houses and walls.

The young man, who never gave us his name and who spoke only when pointing out something, led us upward through a series of wheat fields. Only the barest track existed, and without him we might have wandered off following the promises of its many spurs. Yet we followed only him, our eyes down, choosing our steps carefully.

The wheat climbed up onto the mound, as though onto the back of some huge beast that had slept in this spot for centuries. Across the top, all was billowing yellow, the wheat edging up to frightening drops that, upon inspection, turned out to be appendages of ancient buildings sealed with millen-nia of dust. Near the center of the mound, the young man led us to a deep hole. He pointed downward, as far as the sun could reach, to the layers of crumbled limestone that still held the secrets of Colossae.

As Nur and the young man moved quickly on, I found a place near the edge of the mound with light and air and vision—and I sat with my Bible open to consider all that had taken place here. From the chalky mists of the Lycus and the rumblings of the earth's core, Colossae had molded its golden calf. It was not an idol of riches but of fears, in so many ways the same fears that haunt our lives today: fear of death, fear of abandonment, fear of slavery, fear of freedom. And in their fear, the Colossians had proven vulnerable to voices that would lead them astray.

The world, said the voices, contains much evil. And as you cannot deny the evil in the world, you must in some way deny God. No God who is truly God could allow such evil, so God must be something less, something weaker than God. The only way out, said the voices of Colossae, is submission to the tireless extortions of spirits in charge. Even God must submit, the Colossians were told; how could they hope for a lighter sentence than God?

Hearing all this from Epaphras, Paul must have been silenced for a time. He must have realized that in all he knew to be falsehood there was also much human truth. Life did contain mysteries, life did contain suffering, life did contain a level of evil that strained at every argument he could apply. Yet even as the report from Colossae echoed in his ears, the mystery and meaning of God's will must have echoed in his heart. People can indeed overcome death and darkness, he realized, precisely and only because Christ has already overcome them. People can indeed be delivered from evil, precisely and only because God has already delivered them. We must place our trust in God.

"We do not cease praying for you," Paul wrote to the Colossians, "and asking that you may be filled with the knowledge of God's will." We are all, Paul assures us, "strengthened with every power, in accord with God's glorious might, for all endurance and patience, with joy giving thanks to the Father, who has made you fit to share in the inheritance of the holy ones in light" (Col 1:9-12).

I felt Nur gently touch my shoulder. Then, since I did not or could not respond, she gave it the slightest shake. "Mr.

John," she said—I saw the young man of Colossae standing over her, outlined against the sun—"Mr. John, it is time. We must leave this place and return with you to the city."

Again letting the farmer lead, we took a different path back down toward our car. I felt great reluctance to leave Colossae at all, much less by what was described as the quickest route. Yet there were many thorns among the wheat, and it was impossible to remain in reverie for long. Purple flowers bloomed against the yellow, each armed with its own dagger.

The young man led us to the edge of a cliff, the mound dropping straight to the valley below, with hazy blue mountains in the distance. There was a trail, he pointed out in silence, only a few feet down from where we stood, clinging to the side of the mound. Without effort, he eased himself down onto the trail and reached up his hand for Nur. She gave me an uneasy smile over her shoulder, then let herself be lowered onto the narrow dirt bridge that seemed suspended in the air. As Nur moved to the side in safety, he reached his hand for me.

What did I feel at that moment? And why did I pull back? I was frightened, to be sure, frightened of the thorns and the dirt and the long drop into nothingness. Yet I was also frightened of the young man, of trusting him. Could he hold me the way he'd held Nur? Would he? Or would something in his head or heart let go, and I would die down there on the rocks? I should have trusted him, I knew, but it seemed that I could not.

I waved away the young man's hand. Grabbing onto bushes that seemed well-rooted, I began to lower myself down the stone-and-dirt face of Colossae. In my memory of the moments that followed, I can't say for sure what happened first: whether the bushes pulled out in my desperate hands or my feet began pedaling hysterically toward the edge. Everything I did made it all the worse, for each time my hands clawed into the mountain they only flung up more dirt and rock.

I was glaring at my churning feet when the shadow passed over me. Its coverage was quick and complete, stepping between me and the edge of the mountain. The shadow was the young man, who pressed me hard against the side of the mound until my feet and hands stopped flailing. My heart was beating behind my eyes. But I was on the trail. I stood there on the edge of that cliff in Colossae, smiling stupidly and saying nothing. I did not know what to say.

As usual, Paul knew what to say. It is simple, he tells each of us. It is simple! Touch it. Question it. Test it any way you must. But with all urgency embrace the truth. We must behave as we believe. We must express with our lives what we profess in our liturgies. And we must trust with our every fiber the One who steps between us and destruction, the One who is both liturgy and life.

Pilgrim's Path to the Temple of
Artemis in Ephesus

7

EPHESUS

You are no longer strangers and sojourners, but you are fellow citizens with the holy ones and members of the household of God, built upon the foundation of the apostles and prophets, with Christ himself as the capstone. Through him the whole structure is held together and grows into a temple sacred in the Lord; in him also you are being built together into a dwelling place of God in the Spirit.

Ephesians 2:19-22

For you were once darkness but now you are light in the Lord. Live as children of light.

Ephesians 5:8

I woke abruptly from a troubled sleep, for a moment aware of nothing but the pinpoint of burning in my left forearm. It had been pressed against the bus window as I slept, partially hidden beneath the swaying curtains that kept time as the bus made its way from the Lycus Valley to Ephesus and the sea. Outside the window, I could see we were following yet another valley, a narrow and fertile strip with mountains to the north and south. Judging by the length of the ride, I knew we had followed it on all its unhurried turns, and that the valley had followed the river that had given its name to uses far beyond the geography of the ancient world. The river was known to Paul as the Meander.

The stinging persisted. It seemed such a strange and inexplicable burning that I began to study my forearm, poking and pulling at the skin in hopes it would offer some diagnosis. As I began to shake free of sleep, the whole business began to annoy me. I despised these meaningless discomforts, the kind that ruin an hour, a day, or a week, with little hope of gaining sympathy. Now I was to suffer this crazy burning, just as I prepared to visit the largest archaeological site in Turkey and then catch a boat for Greece. It was not great timing.

I was mystified by the tiny circle of inflammation surrounding the black speck on my forearm. I hadn't noticed it at first, or perhaps the color and swelling were just making their way to the surface. Looking up as though for answers, I found them suddenly in every corner of the bus. Wasps were everywhere, buzzing around the vents on the ceiling, stalking the folds in the curtains. This must have been a normal occurrence here, for my fellow passengers simply stared at the highway and brushed away whatever wasps came near.

Meaningless! I kept raging in silence. It's so meaningless! Some wasp stings me, for no reason, and now every time I move my arm I'm reminded of the injustice. Here I am, trying to feel the presence of God and all I feel is this arm, all I feel is this—this thorn! That's when it struck me: this thorn. Paul had written of a thorn in his flesh, a mysterious affliction that had nagged him throughout his years of doing God's work. Did Paul complain about it? Probably. Did he rage as I did, using words like "meaningless"? Possibly he did. But in the end, what had he written about it? "That I might not become too elated, a thorn in the flesh was given to me, an angel of Satan, to beat me, to keep me from being too elated. Three times I begged the Lord about this, that it might leave me, but the Lord said to me, 'My grace is sufficient for you, for power is made perfect in weakness' " (2 Cor 12:7). Remembering Paul and his thorn, my only wish was that this sting might be mine.

Kusadasi, the city nearest the ruins of Ephesus, proved to be different from any other I'd visited in Turkey. It had grown in the eighteen years since I'd first visited it, when it had seemed to a much younger me a rustic and bohemian resort at the edge of an exotic world. Now it just seemed big, noisy, and bursting at its seams, full of high-rise construction and round-the-clock road repairs.

Ahmed proved to be a different sort of guide as well. He was older than the others, older and considerably more serious. At times he seemed almost sad. As he drove me from the terminal to the Hotel Aydin, he spoke not of Ephesus but of the many things that worried him—Turkey's struggling economy, inflation that hovered at three hundred percent, the sheer difficulty of having a life in the late twentieth century. And he spoke of Islam, the first person to do so in my entire journey through a country that is ninety-nine percent Moslem.

"I work with many Christian groups," he explained, "and I like them very much. Not too many really visit my country or learn anything about the way we live, but many come to Ephesus for the day, by boat from Samos. They ask me questions, and I can see that they are very confused. They ask why I call God Allah—as though God did not have many names in many languages. They ask if I really bow to Mecca five times a day to pray, and if I fall down in the street or go to the mosque." Ahmed smiled. "I tell them I pray, but not just five times a day. God is everywhere—that they understand. So I try to pray wherever I am. I try to pray always.

"And they are amazed, every group and every time, that we honor Abraham as the father of our faith, of all true believers. And that we honor Jesus—your Jesus—as a very great prophet. You see, there are many differences, many things that do keep us apart. But truly, perhaps, the distances are not so very great."

That evening, after Ahmed had left me, I walked out along Kusadasi's bustling waterfront, a kind of wandering park that seemed equally suited to fishermen, strolling seniors, and hundreds upon hundreds of children. The children darted about, bouncing from grass to gravel to concrete, shouting and laughing till their lungs should have burst. Yet all I could think of was Ahmed, of his many worries and also of his faith.

As these children grew to share his worries, would they grow to share his faith? By all evidence, and not for Ahmed alone, the first often seemed unbearable without the second.

May the eyes of your hearts be enlightened, that you may know what is the hope that belongs to God's call, what are the riches of glory in God's inheritance among the holy ones, and what is the surpassing greatness of God's power for us who believe, in accord with the exercise of great might, which God worked in Christ.

Ephesians 1:18-20

After the scant remains of Galatia and Colossae, Ephesus is an embarrassment of riches. In fact, it is alone among Pauline cities in possessing all of four possible elements that can enlighten us about Paul's life and work. Ephesus boasts a rich and recorded history apart from the events of Christianity there. It is today a vast and developed historical site, though scholars insist that all we see is barely a quarter of what remains to be excavated. It offers us a detailed and dramatic rendering of Paul's missionary work, including an encounter with paganism that ended in a riot. And, if we make our peace with scholarly arguments, it gives us in Ephesians a profound and mature Pauline letter, one that casts light on the development of both the Church and Paul himself.

Ephesus also returns us to the sunbright Mediterranean world, with all its pleasures and promises. Though silt from the Cayster River has pushed the sea westward nearly five miles, the city was in ancient times a prominent seaport. Even by Paul's day, this nautical pride of place was only a memory, yet Ephesus continued to operate with a reduced and artificial harbor. Today we see only a low plain stretching to the west and the northwest, to the spot where the Cayster flows into the Aegean Sea.

To the traveler, the Aegean is synonymous with Greece and its starburst of islands, with all its genius and all its beauty. Yet Ephesus had been a successful city thousands of years before the wonders we attribute to the Hellenized world. No fewer than nine thousand years have passed since the first efforts at settlement were made here, and we can see the murals, relief sculptures, and domestic shrines that decorated the place called Catal Huyuk six thousand years before the coming of Christ. A later "Golden Age" of the Hattians lasted until the influx of Indo-European tribes including the Hittites. Famous for their city of Troy (a site identified in the late nineteenth century as being along Turkey's west coast), the Trojans swarmed over the cities of the Hittites beginning in 1180 B.C., ushering in what is known as Anatolia's "Dark Age."

Historians tell us that from the very beginnings of Ephesus, worship of the Great Mother Goddess of Asia was at the very core of its life. The first fortified city on the slopes of Mount Pion was built less than a mile from a sanctuary dedicated to the Anatolian goddess Cybele. Later, wave after wave of Greek-speaking invaders would preserve the cult but change the name to Artemis. The goddess was known universally not simply as Artemis, however; she was known as Artemis of the Ephesians.

The temple erected in honor of this goddess became known as one of the seven wonders of the ancient world, and many over the centuries have called it the grandest of the seven. According to our earliest records, it consisted of two platforms: one holding an altar, the other holding a cult image of Artemis. Archaeologists have uncovered many votive offerings under the limestone at this site.

Ephesus was a wealthy city-state by the time Greek civilization reached its peak. A new temple of Artemis was a reflection of this wealth. The Artemision measured 179 by 375 feet and was the single largest building in the Hellenic world. It was the first monumental structure to be built of marble, with a full 36 of its 127 columns carved with reliefs. In an uncovered area over the ancient altar, the statue of Artemis was placed for worship by her many followers.

It is an ancient Ephesian tradition that a man named Herostatus set fire to the temple on the day Alexander the Great was born. Later Alexander himself offered to bear the expense of rebuilding the place as long as an inscription gave him all the credit. Ever fearful of their goddess and her wrath, the Ephesians refused his offer.

The temple was eventually rebuilt, and it was this version that became known as one of the seven wonders. The new structure added eight additional columns in a third row on the western side and raised the podium to nearly nine feet, with thirteen steps. The columns were a full sixty feet tall, each carved with twenty-four flutes. The altar to Artemis was a large stone table reached by a ramp, its open side looking out toward the sea.

Though not the original stone believed to have fallen from the sky (Acts 19:35), the goddess' cult statue was the rather grotesque figure of a woman with many breasts. Her origins are vague among the shadows of Asia Minor, but she clearly was a symbol of fertility, her motherly attributes multiplied to the extreme. Strangely, she was also viewed as the patron of hunters, a facet carried on by the ancient peoples under her alternate name, Diana. Artemis was often portrayed in the company of two goats, the primary sacrifice offered in her honor.

As history approached the time of Paul, the glories of Greece had dimmed considerably. After the traditional cycle of rule by Alexander's generals and Seleucids, the Romans entered upon the scene, first awarding Ephesus to an ally in nearby Pergamum, and then assuming control themselves. By 29 B.C., the city was the chief metropolis in all Asia, with a sacred precinct dedicated to Rome's divine power as embodied in Caesar Augustus. Fine roads built by the Romans assured the city's continued wealth; it was the banking center for all of western Anatolia.

The Gargantuan Theater
at Ephesus

The ruins of Ephesus must be considered the prince among antiquities. Other sites may have more meaning to individual scholars, and even to individual pilgrims. Yet for magnitude and vision, and the absence of a modern city to distract us, Ephesus not only occupies but creates a class unto itself.

The primary ruins visible today include the harbor, the massive theater, and the agora, or marketplace. That last, in large Greek and Roman cities, was the central point for trade, of course, but also important for the meeting and battling of ideas. It was a place Paul came to know well, first in his preaching to these outposts in Asia, but particularly as his ministry spread at the promptings of the Spirit to the grand cities of ancient Europe.

The harbor of Ephesus was situated along the northern edge of Mount Koressos, with a channel approaching the city from the northwest. A broad and beautiful street led from the harbor to the theater. Known in later years as the Arcadian Way (after Emperor Arcadius who rebuilt it), the thirty-five foot wide avenue featured colonnades fifteen feet deep and bursting with shops on both sides. Great buildings rose up behind every stretch of the colonnaded street. The theater seated no fewer than 24,000 for what to us seems a timeless festival of comedy and drama, and it played an important role in Paul's Ephesian mission as well.

Moving northwest along the marble-paced road, we come to the gymnasium, the baths and the stadium built by Nero on the slopes of Mount Pion. It is believed that Nero began construction during Paul's time in Ephesus, a theory that links his later memories of gladiatorial combat with wild beasts (1 Cor 15:32) to this period. Passing through the city wall at the Koressian gate, we reach the moonscape of fallen stones that once was the Temple of Artemis.

The Acts of the Apostles paints an unusually detailed picture of Paul's work in Ephesus. Though the author gives no indication he was present with Paul in the city, he does serve up a series of dramatic vignettes that reveal a thorough knowledge of the actions and issues involved. Acts tells us, for instance, of Paul's encounter with the "disciples"—believers in Jesus, we assume—who had been baptized in the style of John the Baptist but had never heard of the Holy Spirit (Acts 19:1-7). Both the apostle and the author admired these faithful ones for their new commitment; yet both found deficiency in their failure to recognize the preparatory nature of John's work. Paul had these disciples baptized in the name of Jesus and laid his hands on them, whereupon they received the Holy Spirit with signs of tongues and prophesy. This was the only re-baptism recorded in the entire New Testament.

We see in Acts the expulsion of Paul from the synagogue. He had, we are told, enjoyed its goodwill for three months, being driven from its walls not by the leadership but by unnamed persons who "in their obstinacy and disbelief disparaged the Way before the assembly" (Acts 19:8). Paul led his fellow disciples, his converts, and his curious to a lecture hall operated by one Tyrannus, who allowed the apostle use of it during the hottest part of the day. It is a tribute to these early Christians that they stayed to hear Paul while Tyrannus' students rested out of the heat. Paul, for his part, apparently spent the cooler hours in manual labor. "These very hands," he later reminded the city elders, "have served my needs and my companions" (Acts 20:34).

Surely the most memorable episode recorded from Paul's ministry in Ephesus was the riot of the silversmiths of Artemis. At this point, Christianity, Judaism, paganism, and the Roman empire pulled together into a single dramatic focus. It was fear of angering Artemis (and depriving the silversmiths of income selling replicas of the statue of Artemis) that drove the crowd to hysteria. Into the theater the populace rushed with the rallying cry "Great is Artemis of the Ephesians!" Two of Paul's associates were dragged in as well, and only wise counsel convinced Paul he should not go in after them.

Judaism became part of the battle in the person of Alexander, apparently a leader of the Jewish community. Knowing that Paul was a Jew by birth and fearing that the riot might turn anti-Semitic, Alexander stood up before the crowd and attempted to deny any link between the apostle and his own teachings. Unfortunately for Alexander, the rioters saw before them just another non-believer and shouted him to silence.

After listening to the shouting for two hours, the city secretary broke in to warn that Rome would not tolerate such a disturbance. Privileges accorded the city might be revoked. And besides, the honor of the great goddess was hardly placed in jeopardy by a ragtag band of preachers. If there was a legal problem here, he said, let it be resolved peacefully before the civic assembly.

Though Paul escaped the riot of the silversmiths unharmed, it is clear from this incident that the apostle's nearly three years in Ephesus were fraught with danger. In one of his letters to Corinth, he emphasizes the opportunities for witnessing to the gospel in Ephesus. "A door has opened for me wide and productive for work," he writes, "but there are many opponents" (1 Cor 16:9).

Without doubt, Paul's reference in that same letter (15:32) to battling with wild beasts was a figure of speech. Yet even figuratively, it says much about the volatile nature of his encounters, both with zealous followers of Artemis and with Jews like Alexander who saw him as a threat. There may have even been periods behind bars during Paul's Ephesian ministry; the experts are divided over whether a reference to "many imprisonments" (2 Cor 11:23-27) refers to the years in Ephesus or to some earlier time. Whatever an accurate rendering of these issues might be, we can be certain that Paul felt himself in grave danger here. And we can be equally certain that his gratitude for divine deliverance near the end had a profound impact on the remainder of his life.

For by grace you have been saved through faith, and this is not from you; it is a gift from God; it is not from works, so no one may boast. For we are God's handiwork, created in

Christ Jesus for the good works that God has prepared in ad-
vance, that we should live in them.

Ephesians 2:8-10

I left Ahmed with the car and climbed up through the brambles to a break we had spotted in the chain-link fence. It encircled the eastern entrance to Ephesus, joining with a shoulder-high tangle of thorns to block access to the isolated remains of the Magnesian Gate. There was a narrow path, though my every step produced such sounds of slithering from the underbrush that I preferred not to think who my partners in this pilgrimage might be. I clutched my Bible all the tighter and followed the trail up and under the massive brown stones of the ancient gate.

I had left Ahmed for a quiet consideration of Ephesians, of its place in Paul's life and its meaning in my own. Yet I found myself reading less and thinking more, struggling to come to grips with all the questions nagging at the heels of this letter almost from its earliest reading. Some say it wasn't written to Ephesus at all, and others say it wasn't written by Paul. Why, it hardly seemed worth reading in the shadow of the Magnesian Gate until I had calmed my thoughts on these questions.

Traditionally, Ephesians was viewed as written by Paul to the Church at Ephesus, probably from his prison in Rome. As such, it was grouped with other "captivity epistles," including Philippians, Colossians, and the brief letter to Philemon. Yet the holes in this identification were wide enough to be noticed from the second century onward. At that time, it was theorized that Ephesians was the lost letter to the Laodiceans mentioned in Paul's letter to the Colossians (4:15-17). This seemed to ease tension over similarities between the two writings, but only until their many differences leapt into the fray.

Perhaps, I thought, the "circular" theory might work. After all, the only reference to Ephesus in the entire text (1:1) is missing from the earliest manuscripts. Thus, the letter would be by Paul himself but intended for Ephesus along with other churches. Thus we could understand the strange absence of personal greetings in Ephesians—this from an apostle who found names to drop even in cities he had never visited. Yet Ephesians is not like other letters considered to be circular (Galatians and 1 Peter among them), thus putting this theory to a tough test.

Perhaps the "cover letter" explanation might work, making Ephesians an introduction penned by a disciple for an early collection of Pauline texts. Yet most scholars dismiss this as pure fantasy. After all, they argue, there is nothing introductory about Ephesians. And why would a letter aimed at summarizing and spotlighting Paul's thoughts differ from them on more key issues than most of us care to consider? Why indeed?

It is said by many that Ephesians cannot be Paul's work because it reflects a vision of the Church too mature for the apostle himself. Here in its all-too-brief pages is the Universal Church, not Paul's small congregations that met in homes and played host to itinerant preachers. Here is the Universal Church, coming of age not only in the world's eyes but in its own. Here is the Universal Church, notably lacking in local difficulties and sufferings and errors, notably rich in its vision of the world. Would Paul have even recognized such a Church?

Reading Ephesians with our eyes and hearts open—and particularly reading it pressed against the worn-smooth stones of the Magnesian Gate—we realize that he just might recognize it with greater ease than we do. For once, we see a Church whose identity is less important than its mission, a Church that exists not for its own sake but as a clarion of Christ's saving work in the world. Its mission is its only meaning, and its mission is God's mission—gathering God's people from the diversity of nations and leading them into a unified kingdom. Paul, who saw so clearly that all old alliances had crumbled to dust on that first Easter morning, would have recognized in this kingdom the very light toward which he struggled to steer his life.

In Ephesians, Gentile and Jew are not simply "no more"; they are called by God to be one. It is as though Christ's own prayer for unity—"that they may all be one, as you, Father, are in me and I in you, that they also may be in us, that the world may believe that you sent me" (John 17:21)—had captured the first beachhead in its conquest of the world. There is hope, Ephesians assures us, that all may be one, each time and in every place that we ourselves are one. And not just any hope, it says, but the one true hope, given by a generous God that the unity envisioned by God's Son might one day be complete. On that day, Paul assures us, we will finally see our unity as it is: "one body and one Spirit, as you were also called to the one hope of your call, one Lord, one faith, one baptism, one God and father of all, who is over all and through all and in all" (Eph 4:4-6).

It is said that the Paul we meet in Acts, devoting such time to a single congregation amid its struggles and failures and miracles, could not be the same Paul to whom we ascribe the universal vision of Ephesians. Yet in denying Paul this maturity, this growth, are we not threatening to deny that he could learn from the Church at least as well as he taught it? Are we not threatening to deny that the very things he heard and saw around him, the words and actions of these all-too-specific human beings, might be precisely the words and actions through which God gifted him with this vision? It would be preposterous to deny Paul the very awakenings that even I experienced during the course of my journey, awakenings born of suffering and danger: those moments when, even if only fleetingly, we glimpse the hand of God in what seems the handiwork of man.

"We must thank God for all things."

At first Ahmed's words disoriented me, pulling me out of my thoughts and back into his car as it struggled up the mountain road out of Ephesus. Ahmed had been speaking of Islam, of the many beliefs it shares with Christianity and

Judaism; yet I had drifted again to Ephesians and its portrait of Paul in maturity. Now, hearing only of gratitude to God and lacking any sense of context, I wondered how centuries of theology had ever managed to separate us. And I realized that, despite the illusions of those centuries, none of us had ever been separated by far.

"Yes," I said, "we must thank God." In that moment, my arm responded with the sharpest pinpoint of fire. I knew that this sting would be my thorn for the remainder of my journey with Paul. "For all things," I added.

The Ruins of Paul's Philippi

8

PHILIPPI

My eager expectation and hope is that I shall not be put to shame in any way, but with all boldness, now as always, Christ will be magnified in my body, whether by life or by death. For to me life is Christ, and death is gain.

Philippians 1:20-21

Forgetting what lies behind but straining forward to what lies ahead, I continue my pursuit toward the goal, the prize of God's upward calling, in Christ Jesus.

Philippians 3:13-14

I had long been fascinated by the way Paul traveled to Philippi, especially when I compared it to the way I traveled there. Before my journey, I had pored over ancient and modern maps, had agonized over printed shipping schedules, in search of a way north by sea to Macedonia. Paul engaged in no such agony—a reflection of convenient travel in the Roman world as well as of his reliance on a will and a way other than his own. How Paul went to Philippi, in fact, was intimately related to why he went to Philippi.

He had been moving about with Timothy, the Greek-speaking son of a Jewish woman he had taken as disciple in Lystra—strengthening the churches in faith and number. Yet something was seriously wrong, something Acts of the Apostles accepts so readily that it barely describes what it was, how it felt, or how it worked. We are told that as they traveled through Phrygia and Galatia, Paul and Timothy were forbidden by the Holy Spirit to preach the word in the province of Asia. They tried at one point to preach anyway, attempting to travel to Bithynia, "but the Spirit of Jesus did not allow them" (Acts 16:7). So they went instead to Troas, a coastal city taking its name from the nearby ruins of Troy. It must have seemed they were in Troas for no other reason than to await orders.

The orders came, yet in the strangest form. During the night, Paul experienced a vision. A man appeared before him and implored him with the words, "Come over to Macedonia and help us." Seeing the vision as a call to preach in that region, Paul, Timothy, and apparently Luke, the author of Acts, booked passage immediately.

I remembered the ease of this scriptural booking during my own pre-trip struggles with maps, schedules, and long-distance calls to shipping agents. I was told there were no ships, or there were many ships but they ran irregularly. Oh, there were ships most assuredly, but I'd have to find them when I got to the port. Which day they sailed, well, that was a decision made on the basis of business. It could be done, I was told, but why didn't I just fly to Macedonia? Computers could assure me of that schedule, and no one was going to hold the plane for a day or two because not enough people bought tickets.

I wanted to sail to Macedonia, even if it meant flinging myself off the coast of Turkey till I found a Greek island with connections to Kavalla, the port city Paul knew as Neapolis. I wanted to retrace as closely as possible the sea route Paul had taken, even though for me it involved crossing from one country to another at a time that their tense relations made for awkward links at best. As it turned out, and with an ease Paul would have appreciated, I caught a morning boat from Kusadasi to the island of Samos and discovered a ship sailing for Kavalla the same afternoon. I barely had lunch along the waterfront before it was time to do what I had feared might be difficult or impossible.

The surprising course of events flung me right back to where I should have been all along, reading about the Spirit as it directed and facilitated the movements of Paul and Timothy. They had sailed north from Troas to the island of Samothrace (home of the famed Winged Victory statue in the Louvre) and the next day on to Neapolis. From Neapolis, they had headed inland over the mountains to Philippi on its famous plain, spending what Acts describes as "some time" in the city. This time proved to be long enough to give us a trio of extraordinary vignettes.

Scripture tells us nothing of Paul's approach to Philippi, of whether he began in the synagogue or in the marketplace. Instead, it describes only a quiet Sabbath journey outside the walls to a place along a river where Paul and his associates were told that they would find a place of prayer. That is precisely what they found, a place used for gatherings of women who prayed in the Jewish tradition. One of these women, known to us as Lydia and described as being a dealer in purple cloth, "opened her heart" to the message of life. She and her entire household were baptized in the waters of that unidentified river.

The second vignette takes place on the way to the river, implying that Paul and his followers returned there time and again to pray. A slave girl, whose prophecies had produced no small fortune for her owners, pulled in behind the men and shouted, "These people are slaves of the Most-High God, who proclaim to you a way of salvation" (Acts 16:17). Her oracle strikes us as accurate in spite of itself, yet her persistence became oppressive as a prelude to each day's prayers. Finally, Paul turned to the girl and commanded the spirit that possessed her, by the power of Jesus Christ, to come out. It obeyed.

Stranger even than this deliverance is Scripture's third Philippi vignette. Angered by their loss of income, the owners of the slave girl had Paul and his associate Silas dragged before the magistrates. Accusing the two not only of being disruptive Jews but of advocating customs unlawful for Roman citizens, the owners convinced Philippi's authorities to beat the apostles with rods and throw them into the local prison's innermost cell. We are then told that in the night, as Paul and Silas prayed and sang hymns surrounded by other prisoners, a violent earthquake shook the jail to its foundations, flung open all the doors and shattered every prisoner's shackles. Looking at the devastation wrought by nature, the jailer saw only the freedom of his prisoners and prepared to take his own life in dishonor, until Paul shouted, "Do no harm to yourself; we are all here."

In a remarkable turn on this prison imagery, Paul used the gospel of Jesus to free not only all those held captive, but those who thought they held the keys. The jailer and his entire household were baptized at once, rejoicing "at having come to faith in God." After demanding and, in the end, receiving an apology from the magistrates, Paul and his followers encouraged the believers at Lydia's house and set out for Thessaloniki along the Via Egnatia.

I realized even before my ship pulled into the harbor at Kavalla that these three vignettes teach us much about Paul's work in Philippi, and about his letter to the Philippians. Yet they omit the one fact that intrigued me more than any other, one that perhaps the worldly omnipotence of Rome overshadowed for both Paul and Luke. With the baptisms of Lydia, the jailer and their families, Christianity took its first steps onto the European continent.

> *I give thanks to my God at every remembrance of you, praying always with joy in my every prayer for all of you, because of your partnership for the gospel from the first day until now. I am confident of this, that the one who began a good work in you will continue to complete it until the day of Christ Jesus.*
> Philippians 1:3-6

I stepped off the bus in the heat of the midday sun. It made no sense, of course, to visit the site during the hottest part of the day, yet even the charms of Kavalla's caique-filled harbor could not hold me once I knew Paul's Philippi was less than ten miles away. Even the green, scrub-covered mountains, which began their ascent before the city streets let go, seemed good for little except climbing over on the way to Philippi's vast and hazy plain.

Today's ruins are reached by a blacktopped highway that roughly follows the ancient trade route. There is even a sign to that effect, though I wondered if all travelers up and over these mountains read the unexplained words "Via Egnatia" with an excitement equal to mine. I wondered if all travelers stepping off buses in Philippi knew they were standing at the connecting point of routes that led from the easternmost outposts of the empire all the way to Rome.

If you came from the east in Paul's day—from Syria, Palestine or the faroff lands of Arabia—you made your way overland to Troas and caught a ship, just as the apostle had, to Neapolis. In Philippi you joined what must have seemed a river of traffic, following the Via Egnatia past Amphipolis and across Macedonia with the blue outlines of the Balkan Mountains ever to your north. You walked as far as the Adriatic Sea before catching another ship, this time across the Otranto Straits to Brundisium (modern Brindisi) and the Appian Way across Italy to Rome. Philippi was the fortress guarding the way west, deciding who and what was allowed to pass into the heart of the empire.

When Paul spoke of the city's significance, calling it "the beginning of the gospel" (Phil 4:15), he was echoing the words and works of conquerors before him. The eastward assaults of both Philip and Alexander were empowered by the natural resources of Philippi. It was, we might observe, the spiritual and at times financial resources of Philippi that empowered Paul and his gospel for their westward assault on Europe.

Though their dates are lost in history, the area's earliest Thracian settlers recognized a stronghold when they saw one. The narrow mountain passes made for easy defense, while the game, timber, and minerals made for extended self-sufficiency. There was even an ample water supply, nothing less than a marsh fed by hundreds of mountain springs. These springs gave the city its ancient name: Krenides, or "Little Fountains."

The Phoenicians were apparently the first to intrude on the original Thracian settlements, attracted by the chance to mine Krenides' gold and exploit its lumber for their tireless shipbuilding. The Greeks moved in during the seventh century before Christ, subjecting the area to a series of nondescript rulers until a pair came along who were anything but nondescript. Philip of Macedon took over Krenides in 356 B.C., garrisoned it with his own troops, and renamed its city for himself. History tells us it was the wealth of Philippi that gave Philip the clout to compete with the Athenians and the Persians in both combat and commerce. Troops, after all, conquered territory, and money from territory purchased more troops.

Both Philip and his son Alexander followed the Phoenicians' lead in building ships with Philippi's timber, ferrying their armies to points of conquest all over the ancient world. And the Romans, beginning in 167 B.C., gave every indication of doing much the same.

Macedonia under Rome was divided into four districts, with Philippi in the first district known as a leading colony (Acts 16:12). With Amphipolis on the Strymon River as the district's capital and land stretching as far as the Nestos, Philippi within a decade or two shared with Achaia in Greece many special privileges under the Romans. These were extended even further in 42 B.C., when Antony and Octavian defeated the forces of Brutus and Cassius in the battle immortalized in Shakespeare's *Julius Caesar*. For years, the official coin of the city bore the initials AICVP: Antonii Iussu Colonia Victrix Philippensium (By the Order of Antony the Victorious Colony of the Philippians).

Stones of Via Egnatia Dip into
Lydia's Stream

As a colony, Philippi was left to govern itself, with minimal interference from the district administration in Amphipolis or the provincial control in Thessaloniki. The magistrates of Philippi referred to themselves as "generals" and the citizens thought of themselves, with no shortage of pride, as Romans (Acts 16:20-21).

As I came to understand, walking through the deserted ruins of Philippi that stretched out on both sides of the highway, here was a city-state of classical construction. Its administrative center was atop an acropolis, with its public square and marketplace immediately below. The rectangular forum was located adjacent to the Via Egnatia, complete with a podium used by speakers and two temples holding down the northern corners. A library next to the forum leaves us at least a memory, as do fountains, porticos and monuments. Both the theater and the Roman baths we see were constructed after Paul's time, yet both were built on the ruins of similar structures known by the apostle.

There is even a Roman cistern believed since antiquity to have been the cell that held Paul and the other prisoners until the earthquake set them free. You can look in through the locked iron gate, or you can climb up onto the stones and gaze over the edge into the full extent of the cell. There, under the single remaining piece of arched ceiling, you can pick out fragments of frescos—persuasive indications this otherwise meaningless space was held in some esteem within a century or two of Paul's ministry here.

In the heat of the early afternoon, with direct sun burning the stones and statues white before my eyes, I sat on a fallen column and tried to imagine how the people of Philippi first listened to Paul. What had he told them? And what was it about the way they heard him that made so many find in his message an echo in their own hearts?

Over the centuries, the Philippians had embraced every known religion and cult—the Thracian god Liber Pater and goddess Bendis, the Greek goddess Athena, the Roman gods

Jupiter and Mars. Many, too, had worshiped the Anatolian mother goddess Cybele and the Egyptian divinity Isis. Yet for all of this idolatry, and perhaps even because of it, many in Philippi had developed a great and painful skepticism about organized religion. These were people desperately weary of falsehood, desperately weary of exploitation by temple charlatans and artful profiteers. They longed for something real, something they could poke and prod and hold up to the light, something that no matter how they turned it kept assuring them it was true. When Paul moved among them speaking of Jesus, they knew they had found that something.

Paul's ministry clearly made an impression on the Philippians, for by the time he wrote to them from a Roman prison he was at peace not only with all he had accomplished but with all he heard of their progress. Theirs were only minor problems, not the major errors he addressed with passion in Galatia, Colossae, or Corinth. Paul could use his letter as a shimmering herald of gratitude and joy, built on the hope of seeing them all again in the promised light of their Lord.

He could speak with calm, too, of his own life of suffering and travel, the life that for a brief time the Philippians had shared. Some days, as he wrote, release from prison seemed incredibly near. Other days, it seemed that his release was beyond the faintest hope, with execution the only likely outcome. Either way, he assured them, he would rejoice. Either way, he would sing God's praises. For he had come into a new strength and a new sufficiency, based not on qualities of his own but on trust in God.

Death, Paul promises, is unity with Christ—a unity we are called by Christ and in Christ to mirror in our lives here on earth. "If there is any encouragement in Christ," he writes, "any solace in love, any participation in the Spirit, any compassion and mercy, complete my joy by being of the same mind, with the same love, united in heart, thinking one thing" (Phil 2:1).

Rejoice in the Lord always. I shall say it again: rejoice!
Philippians 4:4

"Oh yes," the guard said, practically leaping out of his
booth at the entrance to the ruins and leading me by the arm
to the highway. It had taken me several attempts at breaking
the language barrier, several chances to try my smattering
of words in a tangle of tongues, with no effect beyond self-
mortification. Finally, just as I contemplated the international
shrug of surrender, all my poorly chosen phrases seemed to
connect in the guard's mind, his entire face brightened, and
he stood pressing me onward up the highway. "Yes," he said
almost breathlessly. "This road you walk. Stream Lydia."

I had pushed at the boundaries of Philippi all afternoon,
following each strip of crushed stones on the hunch it might
be the Via Egnatia. I had climbed over every wall I could
identify, and crawled out through anything that might have
been a city gate. Each time, in weeds higher than my head,
I had run up against a rusting fence marking the end of the
site. Once, on instinct, I'd even climbed the fence. This had
only deposited me in the center of bedraggled sheep, guarded
by one sleeping shepherd and one extremely awake dog. I had
no trouble climbing back over the fence.

Now I was on my way to finding what I had sought without knowing it since first setting foot in Philippi. The highway led out away from the site and in away from the sea,
stretching off in panoramas to the mountains beyond the plain.
Somewhere nearer those mountains lay the Macedonian town
of Drama; yet here on the highway tracing the Via Egnatia
out of Paul's Philippi, I had just about all the drama I could
stand.

Off to my left, in among the brown and yellow patch-
work of fields, a strand of green hedged closer and closer with
every step I took. It even seemed to feel cooler, despite the
heat rising from the near-liquid blacktop, especially when I'd
pause at the top of a hill to let the breeze work its way across

my drenched shirt and pants. Less than a mile past the last visible ruins of Philippi, the highway curved through a tiny cluster of buildings with a bright green oasis to the left. A small sign stood on the shoulder, ready to flag down the fervent or the simply curious. All it read was: "Lydia."

The trail that led off the highway carried me right through the center of a tiny gift shop stocked, I'm certain, with no more than fifty religious postcards and several bottles of lukewarm cola. The woman behind the counter pointed off to the right past her doorway. "Church," she said. And then she pointed off to the left, whispering a variant on the word I longed to hear. "Reever."

The church turned out to be locked, yet I reacted with relief. At that moment, I knew, no church in all the world could feed me what I needed to eat.

The shade was as good as a shower, bathing me with cool air amid the sound of rushing water. The trail led through lush greenery to a shadowed spot at the water's edge. Huge white stones slipped down into the stream and rose up as though newly baptized on the other bank. These stones were all that remained of the glorious Via Egnatia. This stream was all that remained of a single moment in history that propelled faith in Jesus onto a new continent and into the heart of a new world.

This was undeniably a place of prayer, precisely as Paul and his followers had described it. It was that rarity among the earth's antiquities, a place of prayer that remained one. Philippi seemed a lifetime lost in my past, Thessaloniki a lifetime concealed in my future. Only this place existed for me, only this place and these cooling waters and these deep, caressing shadows.

I could imagine Lydia here, praying among the women of Philippi with fervor, with confidence, with a surrender I have never seen among men. And I could imagine Paul stepping into their circle, in every sense a messenger with urgent and joyous news. He had taught them and he had touched them. And he had baptized them, along with the millions who are their legacy, into new life. Then—and this I could imagine most clearly of all—he had given them a song to sing.

It was a hymn Paul had learned years earlier. Where had he learned it? Perhaps among the Christians of Antioch. Perhaps among the believers in Jerusalem. Perhaps he had felt it enter his life as far back as Damascus, enter his life with that light, coming to take on words and music only as the years accumulated. It was a hymn about a king.

No, not a king, a god. And not just a god but the one true God, creator and sustainer of all. And this God, in Paul's hymn, in his single most dizzying mystery, came to live among us. Not as the pagan deities had pretended to, parading about in the trappings of flesh and blood. No, this God came to live as a human being, to breathe and thirst and question and suffer, even to die as one of us. This God sought never to live as the equal of God, always to live and finally to die as slave to all he ruled—to us who so rarely see God for what he is. In the surrender and sacrifice of Jesus, God raised him up from among all, raised him to a place above all places and made his the name above all names. God renewed the length and breadth and depth of creation with a single proclamation so simple, yet so transforming, that, buried two thousand years in our past, it remains the only present we truly possess. It brings us to our knees. It ennobles our lips. It fills us with life and hope and strength and meaning—each time we proclaim, as Lydia once did on the banks of a nearly forgotten stream, that Jesus Christ is Lord.

Excavation of Main Street in
Roman Thessaloniki

9

THESSALONIKI

*Concerning times and seasons, you have no need for any-
thing to be written to you. For you yourselves know very well
that the day of the Lord will come like a thief at night. When
people are saying "peace and security," then sudden disaster
comes upon them, like labor pains upon a pregnant woman, and
they will not escape.*

1 Thessalonians 5:1-3

*May the God of peace make you perfectly holy and may
you entirely, spirit, soul and body, be preserved blameless for
the coming of our Lord Jesus Christ.*

1 Thessalonians 5:23

The taxi driver in his glistening Mercedes couldn't believe I wasn't fluent in at least one of his languages. That I
couldn't speak his native Greek—well, that he could understand. But German struck him as a tongue any intelligent
traveler should possess. With increasing delight, he ran me
through the remainder of his list, laughing each time I said
"No": Bulgarian, Yugoslavian, Albanian. I think the last was
a private joke, since Albanian refugees were streaming into
Greece on the very day of our ride.

The driver was proud of his fluency and his success. He
explained both to me as we moved in comfort through the
highrises of Thessaloniki, conversing in a new tongue constructed from German, bits of Italian, and plenty of sign language. I couldn't help noticing that the street signs marking

"Bulgaria" or "Yugoslavia" seemed as unaware of their exoticism as signs for Elm or Maple back home. Thessaloniki sits with some satisfaction at the crossroads of its own little world, with enough traffic today to make yesterday and tomorrow seem insignificant.

As we drove through the midday heat, with the air conditioner blowing a frigid cyclone inside the car, the driver gave me a sales pitch on his life. He had made his money in Germany, working several jobs while living on as close to nothing as possible. Finally, like some trader riding the Wall Street tiger, he had managed to leap off, buy the one symbol that said it all, and come home to Thessaloniki. He spent his days ferrying corporate high-rollers from the airport to the major regional headquarters downtown. Why had he ever looked at me—thoroughly rumpled from boats and buses, my duffel bag white with dust—and thought to ask if I needed a ride?

I told my driver of my quest for Paul as soon as we started talking, so he took every opportunity to point out historical sites he thought would mean something to me. Sadly, his grasp of history, like Thessaloniki's, seemed mightily indistinct. Anything built between 1,000 B.C. and 500 A.D. qualified as far as he was concerned. And even with the window opened wide, he didn't have much to point out. By the time we reached my hotel near the waterfront, I was convinced the driver said it all about Thessaloniki, and that the world of Paul and his Thessalonians would end up listed "missing in action." The present was simply too good, too big, too driven for my driver and a million others just like him.

To make matters worse—much worse—I finally managed in Thessaloniki to get a phone connection home. I had tried from hotels and telephone headquarters all over Turkey. Yet despite assurances that such connections were easy, I'd gotten only an odd assortment of clicks and whistles and beeps leading back to the drawnout "shhhhhh" of sleep. From the shimmering new PTT in Thessaloniki, however, I dialed the codes as instructed and the call went through with the ease of ordering a pizza. It was shocking to hear members of my family at the other end of the line, since I had begun to despair of ever reaching them. Almost as soon as the connection was made, I looked back on that former feeling with nostalgia.

Things were going badly, my wife reported. At seven months pregnant, she was feeling horrible. She said I should have known it would be like this and I should never have left her. The children? During the first few days of my absence they had cried a lot and asked how many days till I came home. But then they had given up and stopped crying and started getting angry. Now all they talked about was the vacation I'd canceled to go off on this journey. Now the family couldn't go to the beach. Now we'd be having this baby. And then school would start and then. . . . Individually, at three different levels of maturity, the children confirmed their mother's report. They suggested I just stay wherever I was and they'd learn to get along without me. Worst of all, in a way that even my feverish "I love you" couldn't change, they seemed to be learning already.

I had to sit for several minutes before I could walk over to the cashier's window. I was shaking as I paid the $12, or was it $18? What was the exchange rate anyway? And what did it matter? I walked out into the modern streets of Thessaloniki, struggling to resist the temptation to book the first flight west in hopes of reaching my family a day, an hour, even a minute earlier. Everything inside me knew better, and everything inside me knew why I was here. But the thought that "here" was Thessaloniki, and that "here" would probably hold so little for me, brought hysteria all the closer.

I had tried to assure my family that only Athens and Corinth remained, but they hadn't given me the chance. Now all I could do was assure myself.

"Home soon." That's what I'd told my three-year-old, almost idiotically, over and over, until it seemed more for me than for her. "Home soon." Those two words became my comfort and my prayer as I tried to remember Paul in a city that had lost its memory. Home soon, I kept whispering as I walked. Home soon!

> *We ought to give thanks to God for you always, brothers loved by the Lord, because God chose you as the firstfruits for salvation through sanctification by the Spirit and belief in truth. To that end God has called you through our gospel to possess the glory of our Lord Jesus Christ.*
>
> 2 Thessalonians 2:13-14

As any Thessalonian should have known, the city in truth has much to remember. In ancient times, as now, Mount Olympus rose in the southern distance, home to the gods of the Hellenistic world. Concealed in forests at its base was the Pierian Spring, where the Muses were given life, and Orpheus came forth into the light. The city Paul would come to know was founded by Cassander, one of Alexander's generals, and named after his wife—half-sister to the conqueror himself and the last surviving member of Macedonia's royal family.

Thessaloniki was for centuries the most populous city in all Macedon, earning praise from sources as diverse as the geographer Strabo and the poet Antipater. Xerxes paid it more pragmatic praise, using it as his base of operations for his invasion of Europe. One ancient saying tied all the city's gifts into a single impressive bundle: ''So long as nature does not change, Thessaloniki will remain wealthy and prosperous.''

Straddling the Via Egnatia on its route from Asia to Europe and serving as Macedonia's primary outlet to the sea, the city was poised for great things from the fifth century B.C. onward. At that time, its harbor was twice as large as the one we see today, with silt from the Vardar River filling in vast portions of it over the centuries. Even in Paul's day, river silt has enclosed the western end of the city with a large lake and marshes infested with mosquitoes.

In these Walls, Paul's
Thessalonians Awaited Christ

The last stronghold of the Antigonid Dynasty fell before the Roman war machine in 167 B.C., letting Alexander's united empire be divided into four parts with Thessaloniki the administrative center of one of them. When Macedonia was consolidated as a province two decades later, Thessaloniki became the captial as well as the official residence of the proconsul, the governor appointed by Rome. Further dividends accrued to the city in the wake of its wager on Antony and Octavian at the Battle of Philippi. As the victorious Octavian moved toward declaring himself Caesar Augustus, he declared Macedonia an imperial province with only occasional visits by Roman troops. A new age of freedom and security had begun.

Paul noted all these things when he arrived in Thessaloniki from Philippi, probably around 50 A.D. In the city itself, he found an opportunity to preach effectively of Jesus amid the mix of Jews, Greek followers of Judaism, and affluent women who attended the synagogue out of curiosity. This same cosmopolitan mix impressed Paul with its mobility, striking him as a promising springboard for the spread of his gospel (1 Thess 1:8).

We have no record of how long Paul stayed in Thessaloniki, but we know how much he accomplished there. We know he had enough time to establish a clientele for his tentmaking trade, using his own hands to keep his ministry going. We know he won a significant following among the Gentiles and made some headway among his fellow Jews. We know he had enough time to receive two gifts from the Philippians (Phil 4:16), to begin formation of an important Church and possibly even to visit Illyricum on what is today the Dalmatian coast (Rom 15:19).

Yet for all this, we know Paul's time in Thessaloniki was by his reckoning not enough. Read with a focus on the apostle himself, the two letters we have to the Thessalonians are touching in their desire to fill in blanks that he wished he had not been forced to leave, to correct misunderstandings he would have addressed in person had he been given the chance. Acts of the Apostles tells us in some detail of the events that abruptly ended the promising ministry in Thessaloniki.

As in Philippi, and for many of the same reasons, Paul's message of a personal God—a loving Father, a redeeming Son, an empowering Spirit—struck a deep and vital chord in Thessaloniki. Even if the city's pagan past made for the very problems later addressed in Paul's letters (sexual indulgence from the cults of Dionysus and Orpheus, misconceptions about the afterlife from worship of the Egyptian gods Isis and Serapis), it also made for a population ready to think, to worship, to live in an entirely new way.

An additional element in the Thessalonian story is supplied by the women of the city, who apparently enjoyed far greater freedom here than did their counterparts in Athens or Corinth. They were drawn initially to Judaism, finding both its theology and its ethics far more sensible than anything concocted in the name of pagan deities. With the arrival of Christianity, these same women saw even in its broadest outlines an emancipation far more complete than any promised them in the past. The equality we know Paul described to them—of slaves and masters, of Gentiles and Jews, and women and men—struck these listeners with a power they'd never dared hope for in any temple or synagogue.

As usual, Paul's message was rightly perceived as a threat to the existing order. And as usual, this perception began precisely where Paul began: in the synagogue. "This is the Messiah, Jesus," he told the Jews and proselytes gathered within its walls, "whom I proclaim to you" (Acts 17:3). The synagogue leaders responded in a manner familiar to all lovers of the way things used to be, wherever in two thousand years Christianity has come to live. "These people who have been creating a disturbance all over the world have now come here," they said. "They act in opposition to the decrees of Caesar and claim instead that there is another king, Jesus." In stirring up the crowds and putting the local magistrates on notice, the synagogue leaders were repeating nearly two decades after his trial before Pilate the charges brought against Jesus himself.

The resolution of this crisis was a compromise that seemed satisfactory to everyone—everyone, that is, except Paul. When the leaders of the local Church hustled Paul and Silas out of Thessaloniki for Beroea to the southwest, they preserved themselves and their fellow believers from persecution. They also relieved the magistrates of a crisis certain to grow more unsavory by the minute.

Yet the two letters portray a Paul who left Thessaloniki virtually with his arms outstretched, no doubt with his lips burning for one last chance to teach and touch the people. "Night and day we pray beyond measure," Paul would write (1 Thess 3:10-12), "to see you in person and to remedy the deficiencies of your faith. Now may God, our Father, and our Lord Jesus direct our way to you, and may the Lord make you increase and abound in love for one another and for all, just as we have for you."

The one who calls you is faithful, and he will accomplish it.
1 Thessalonians 5:24

Undistracted, as it were, by Pauline sites to visit in modern Thessaloniki, I let myself be drawn deeper and deeper into the lines of Paul's two letters to the Christians there. I was certain the letters were written with love. There could be no doubt they were written with correction. Yet above all, both were written in the spiritual frenzy of a community expecting nothing less than the coming of the Lord. Even a casual reader can sense Paul's struggle to present an event he saw at the heart of his own conversion as the essential heart of the Christian mission to and in the world.

Somehow, as I stalked the streets and reread these letters each time I rested my legs, Paul's yearning for his Thessalonians and my yearning for my family took on a kind of
oneness I could not begin to explain. There was little theology to support such a relationship, and no reasonable psy-
chology either. Yet I was convinced, as I whispered the
infantile words "Home soon," that my prayer in what seemed
to be exile echoed the prayers of Paul. Even as his written
words calmed me from near-hysteria, they made me long to
be home all the more.

Generally, Paul's Thessalonian correspondence is recognized as his earliest that is preserved for us. As such, and even
more intriguingly, these letters represent the oldest written
record of faith in the risen Jesus. Later controversies over doctrine or administration find no place to rest their heads in
Paul's Church of Thessaloniki. Indeed, this barely seems a
"Church" at all. The Thessalonians we sense at the receiving end are a loosely organized gathering of believers, high
on anxiety and low on planning in the perceived onrush of
God's final victory. Paul senses in their very passion for
Christ's return the need for further instruction, seeing perhaps for the first time the limitations of familiar apocalyptic
imagery in foreshadowing the final chapter of God's history.

The first Thessalonian letter struck me in many ways as
the more interesting, not to mention the more universally acknowledged as being from Paul's own hand. The love he con-
veys, the responsibility he accepts for the people he left so
abruptly comes through in virtually every line.

Paul's ethical teachings in 1 Thessalonians grapple with
a serious problem at the core of Christian expectation: how
we must live in the light of God's approaching triumph. The
apostle learned from Timothy that some in the community
were using the promised Parousia as an excuse for adultery
and other sexual excess. Not only did Paul see the conflict
between this supposedly Christian belief and the most basic
tenets of Christian life; he began to see that all apocalyptic

expectation must be lived in obedience to Jesus' own teaching and example. "God did not call us to impurity but to holiness," he wrote. "Therefore, whoever disregards this, disregards not a human being but God" (1 Thess 4:7-8).

This teaching, however, seems but prelude to the central assurance we believe inspired Paul to write his letter. We are told that as time passed, a creeping disappointment worked its way through the Christian community in Thessaloniki, undermining both its faith and its fervor. The pitch of expectancy had been too high for a Savior who might not come for months, for years, even for centuries. Additionally, many Christians had gone to their graves in precisely this frenzy of expectation, leaving their loved ones to fear the dead might be overlooked when the day of the Lord finally came. This was clearly a theological issue, a question of what scholars call eschatology. Yet when Paul addressed it, he seemed far less concerned with theory than with the sufferings of people in pain.

Surely, Paul writes with supreme consolation, the God who proved faithful throughout past ages, who revealed love in the fullness of time by sending the Son will forget not a single face among those who have ended their lives in the service of the Lord. Surely, the same grace and power that raised Jesus on that first Easter will lift up the faithful dead and reunite them with the faithful living, will enfold them all in a single embrace. "For if we believe that Jesus died and rose," Paul writes, "so too will God, through Jesus, bring with him those who have fallen asleep" (1 Thess 4:14).

If indeed the two Thessalonian letters are Paul's earliest written declarations of faith, they clearly show him wrestling with a line of thought and a mode of expression he would over time abandon completely. Particularly in 2 Thessalonians, with its prophecies of the "man of lawlessness" who would rise to power before the Son of Man could return, Paul seems to be dabbling in the same symbolic envisioning that fired the Book of Daniel in the Old Testament and the Book of Revelation in the New. Into our own day, people who know little else of Paul lift these troubling passages from 2 Thessalonians and weave them with prophecies real and imagined into a personal timetable of the Apocalypse.

This misunderstanding, and at its worst this manipulation, of our certainty Christ will come again is precisely what terrified Paul gazing into the future of the Church by way of his beloved in Thessaloniki. People abandoning morality. People refusing to work. People immobilized by fear, whether for their loved ones or for themselves. Paul introduced in these two letters, and developed dramatically later on, his insistence that the only true meaning of our world's future lies in our shared past with a promise: the life, death and resurrection of Jesus.

When Jesus walked among us, he spoke often of the end times. He reserved for these discussions, in fact, a passion we sense in no other teachings except those about his Father. Jesus did tell his listeners of signs that would foreshadow the end. Yet he also assured them there could be no calculation, that only his Father knew the final hour, and that when it came it would be as a thief in the night. Paul unabashedly borrowed this image from the tradition he had absorbed, using it to caution the Thessalonians.

The Jesus Paul knew from tradition spoke often of the kingdom of God. Yet with all we think we know of this kingdom, and with all Jesus had to say about it, perhaps "kingdom" is not the best word at all. "Rule" might describe more fully what Jesus had in mind, the sheer outbreak of God at the center of creation.

As Jesus spoke of God's coming triumph, all then as now heard in their own way. Some heard Jesus say this rule was "at hand" and decided this meant close in time. They gathered their families in darkened corners and awaited the end with trembling. Others looked to their own hands and decided Jesus meant close in distance, as though the rule of God was something so tangible, so real, they could touch it as easily as they could touch Jesus. Others heard Jesus say the rule of God was "in their midst"—and some must have looked around themselves sadly, wondering "Where? Here? Now?" Still others heard Jesus say the rule of God was "within them." As both factual and transcendent statement, it would remain undeniably, exultantly true.

From the traditions of Jesus that he knew and from his own burning awareness of the future's swift approach, Paul pressed the promises of Apocalypse toward the only response he judged acceptable for the Christian: a life lived in waiting within, quite essentially, a life truly lived. He leaped to the heart of the Christian contradiction and came back bearing as fine a balance as anyone in two thousand years. Paul's balance is dramatic. Paul's balance is exhilarating. Paul's balance is almost too much of a challenge to live in our daily lives.

Because of all that is not yet, Paul teaches, we are called to live it all already. The story of God's coming triumph must be written in our faces now, written so large that even the blind can read it. The glow from God's future must be reflected in our eyes now, visible to all who chance or dare to gaze into them. Not yet Christ's coming may truly be; yet we are called to receive Christ now.

We have the assurance of Paul. We have the promise of God. We will indeed be home soon.

The Parthenon Reminded Paul of
All Reason Could—and Could
Not—Achieve

10

ATHENS

You Athenians, I see that in every respect you are very reli-
gious. For as I walked around looking carefully at your shrines,
I even discovered an altar inscribed, "To an Unknown God."
What therefore you unknowingly worship, I proclaim to you.
Acts 17:22-23

For I am not ashamed of the gospel. It is the power of God
for the salvation of everyone who believes: for Jew first, and then
Greek. For in it is revealed the righteousness of God from faith
to faith.
Romans 1:16-17

That Athens became a city of memories for me is not
without foundation in Paul; for by the time he walked its
streets, preached in its marketplaces, and argued before its
judges, Athens had become a city of memories for itself as
well. We cannot understand Paul's enticing ministry here if
we insist on setting him down in the company of Plato and
Socrates. Their glorious discourses, along with so much that
we revere of Greek drama and architecture, were centuries
in the past. If we as visitors catch ourselves wandering blankly
through legacies of a far grander time, we should feel a certain kinship with the Athenians of Paul's day. The more honest
among them must have felt they were doing much the same.

Nonetheless, entering Athens after traveling south from
Macedonia, the apostle clearly encountered a world quite unlike any he had visited so far. Unlike the cities of Asia Minor,

whose Greco-Roman veneer barely covered a dark and fearful past, Athens knew to its very core it had done something
extraordinary to lead humankind into the light. Its breathtak-
ing buildings, memories of an age named for the ruler Pericles,
were testimony to Paul that the people of Athens had glimpsed
something of the one true God. Yet for all the Athenians' insight and vision, the idols that decorated every available space
assured Paul they had never seen God clearly.

As I climbed atop the Areopagus or joined the tourist
flow through the Acropolis, I found myself wishing Paul had
written a letter to these Athenians. What a marvelous work
that would have been! Fully in its pages, Paul would have
set down the history of God's revelation—a thousand lines
of seemingly unrelated thought, all weaving through the
shadows of the past to converge in the future upon the Son.
Fully, Paul would have explained, reasoned, and argued that
just as the law of Moses had for the Jews been preparatory
to God's final gathering, so for them was their light, their vision of the creator, and their efforts to pay their creator homage. We have no ''Letter to the Athenians,'' sadly, and no
indication that Paul ever wrote one.

What we have is the record in Acts of the Apostles, less
than a chapter pressed between Paul's adventures in Thessaloniki and what we know to have been his extended ministry in Corinth. Corinth, by Paul's time, was a larger and more
powerful city than Athens—so perhaps Acts' treatment is
simply reflective of that. Yet its brief descriptions of the
apostle's activities and its rendering of his speech to the
Areopagus tantalize us with pieces missing from the puzzle.

The Athens of Paul is described as a ''city full of idols''
(Acts 17:16), a vision the apostle found intolerable both as
a Christian and as a Jew. Never passing up a chance to live
out his commission, Paul is said to have debated with worshipers in the synagogue (though presumably not about the
idols) and with whoever happened to be in the public squares.
This last group included Epicurean and Stoic philosophers,

whose legacies of thought Paul had confronted often in his travels through the Hellenistic Roman world.

The reaction of Athenians in the squares was quite different from the response generally ignited in the synagogue: "You bring some strange notions to our ears," they told him. "We should like to know what these things mean." The author of Acts is noting Athens' reputation for listening to innovative ideas, a willingness at the heart of its most profound achievements. Yet he feels no need to pay these people homage, seeing them through the critical eyes of Paul's preaching. "All the Athenians," says Acts, "as well as the foreigners residing there used their time for nothing else but telling or hearing something new" (Acts 17:21).

Something new is indeed what they heard from Paul, particularly those who followed him as he was led before the court known to Athenians as the Areopagus. Meeting either on the hill of that name or, as they began to do later, in the nearby Royal Stoa, these men and all who gathered around them heard one of the most remarkable, and most controversial, presentations in Paul's entire missionary career.

It is argued by some that Paul's Areopagus speech is conclusively "non-Pauline," that its reliance on Greek poets instead of Scripture is contrary to all we know of the apostle's character, and that its references to God lack the anchoring focus on Christ. Jesus is not even mentioned by name in the speech, though a clear reference to his resurrection in the past and his role in the future turns up at the close. It is tempting to imagine Luke inventing this speech for Paul. Indeed, if Paul didn't assure us elsewhere that he spent time in Athens (1 Thess 3:1), we might imagine the author inventing that as well. When full consideration is given the Areopagus speech, this is a temptation we should resist.

For one thing, the address carries distinct echoes of the defense presented by Paul and Barnabas at Lystra to the locals preparing to worship them as gods. In Lystra and more fully in Athens, Paul steps away from reliance on Old Testa-

ment prophecies which, after all, would have meant nothing
to his listeners, and centers his argument on humankind's
yearning for God. It is a yearning, Paul argues, built not upon
our desire, need, or ability to find God but on a loving God's
deepest and most empowering wish: to be found by us in creation. "God made from one the whole human race to dwell
on the entire surface of the earth," Paul proclaims. "And God
fixed the ordered seasons and the boundaries of their regions,
so that people might seek God, even perhaps grope for and
find God, though indeed God is not far from any of us" (Acts
17:26-27).

Paul quotes a Greek poet from his native Cilicia to echo
one of his own favorite themes: "We, too, are his offspring."
Yet he uses this quote as a foundation to attack the city's worship of idols and prepare his audience for fuller teaching on
the coming of the Lord. Divinity, he says, is no image to be
fashioned by hands or imagination, no image to be formed
from gold, silver, or stone. God is a spirit, a power, a being
who has led all peoples forth, each people through its own
version of exile, into a land of promise through and with and
in Jesus Christ. Offspring we are, Paul teaches the Athenians, but offspring in need of repentance. For the Son of God
has been appointed, as confirmed by his resurrection on the
first Easter, to come again and "judge the world with justice."

Those who read the Areopagus speech, even read it atop
the Areopagus itself, and insist Paul could not have given it,
must be insisting on vocabulary when they should be seeking
meaning. They are missing the fact that the speech mirrors
the pattern of biblical revelation in all its fullness: God as creator, God as sustainer, and God as judge of all. And they
are overlooking the fact that this same Paul, in his longest
and most profound letter, sounded the very warning it is argued he never would have issued amidst the remembered glory
of Athens.

"What can be known about God is evident to them, because God made it evident to them," Paul would write to the
Romans (1:19-23). "Ever since the creation of the world,

God's invisible attributes of eternal power and divinity have been able to be understood and perceived in what God has made. As a result, they have no excuse, for although they knew God, they did not accord God glory as God, or give God thanks. Instead, they became vain in their reasoning, and their senseless minds were darkened. While claiming to be wise, they became fools and exchanged the glory of the immortal God for the likeness of an image.''

> *The God who made the world and all that is in it, the Lord of heaven and earth, does not dwell in sanctuaries made by human hands because God needs anything. Rather it is God who gives to everyone life and breath and everything.*
>
> Acts 17:24-25

If, as Paul writes, it is God who gives us ''life and breath and everything,'' then God has been exceptionally generous in what was given to Athens. Throughout the city's long history, the idea that the creator is visible in creation has been understandable to many who walked its sacred ways and bathed themselves in its sacred light. For those guided not by maps but by the teachings of Paul, it is understandable even now.

Athens' origins are a tapestry more of myths than recorded events, beginning with the scant remains of a people called the Pelasgians and leading up to a half-legendary hero related to Hercules by the name of Theseus. Over the centuries, the very names of the powerful people who shaped Athens came into use to describe their political kin. Draco, for instance, used the death penalty to punish even minor thefts—giving us the grim designation ''draconian.'' Solon ushered in new freedom for all classes, inspiring us who live in a variant on Greek democracy to call all lawmakers ''solons.'' In other areas, the Athenians at their grandest set down the measurements by which all future attempts would be judged: Socrates, Plato, and Aristotle in philosophy, Aeschylus, Sophocles, and Euripedes in drama.

The Athens Paul saw before him was, we are told, in many ways the vision of a single man and a single thirty-year period of history. Between 460 and 429 B.C., Pericles rebuilt a city largely sacrificed to defeat the Persian ruler Xerxes, rebuilt it more beautifully than even its past admirers could imagine. From the Age of Pericles, we have virtually all the Athens Paul would have known, and virtually all the Athens busloads of visitors from around the world consider worth visiting.

By walking (and in some cases climbing) relatively short distances in the center of a sprawling modern city of four million people, we can actually add our footsteps to those of the apostle at the three major sites of his ministry here. The Agora, the Areopagus, and the Acropolis form a triumvirate of our shared Christian past.

It was in the Agora, or public market, that Paul disputed with the people of Athens, including the well-entrenched Epicurean and Stoic philosophers. The Stoics, in fact, spent so much time debating among the columns of the Stoa Poikele that they actually took their name from it. The Royal Stoa, another column-lined walkway with shops and offices at the back, was built near the end of the Periclean age and had been the spot favored by Socrates. As this building was the official seat of the king, or archon, other public buildings rose nearby. The two-story Stoa of Attalus, the Bouleuterion to seat the 600-member council, the round Tholos to seat city administrators, the Metroon to house the archives, all had been standing for centuries by the time of Paul.

Though the Agora was to both Greek and Roman a place of government and commerce, its builders passed up few opportunities to worship gods, goddesses, and Athens' broad selection of heroes. Today, the Thesion on the Agora's highest point is one of the market's most visible buildings, named after Theseus but actually dedicated to Hephaestus, the god of craftsmen. The Temple of Apollo was close at hand, as was the Temple of Zeus and Athena, the Temple of Ares, and a host of altars constructed to Zeus and the city's nearly deified early heroes.

It was Paul's preaching in this marketplace that landed him before the Areopagus. Today all we have is a hill of white stone, its limestone perilously smooth from centuries of visitors climbing to its top for a dramatic view of the Acropolis. Though the so-called Areopagites met in the Royal Stoa beginning in the first century, most scholars believe Paul was brought to the hill itself to defend his proclamations.

In a sense, the Areopagus formed the "brain trust" of Athens. Though stripped of many powers as far back as the fifth century B.C., the body continued to issue licenses for teachers and other propagators of ideas. What their discussions amounted to was a volatile mix of philosophy, theology, and politics. Confronted by the message of salvation through faith in Jesus Christ, it seems that even some of its members joined other Athenians in believing. Scripture records the name of one of Paul's converts as Dionysius the Areopagite (Acts 17:34).

The Acropolis, Athen's best-known landmark, and for many the ultimate symbol of Greece at its grandest, surely must have made an impression on Paul. As a lifelong student of Hellenistic thought, he must have felt some excitement striding along the Panathenaic Way through the busy Agora and between the massive retaining walls of the Acropolis itself. Yet he must have been repulsed as well, for the entire hilltop seemed to throb with idols believed by the Greeks to sustain their very life.

Paul would have seen the Temple of Athena Nike on a rise to his right, and the large, much newer statue of Agrippa straight ahead of him. Turning to his right, he would have faced the Propylaea, the massive gateway to the Acropolis. Columns lined his route past the Pinakotheke, or picture gallery, columns alive and noisy with worshipers carrying animals chosen for sacrifice. Emerging from the Propylaea, Paul would

have seen the graceful Erechtheion to his left and the looming spear-carrying statue of Athena Promachos directly above
his head. In his path, drawing his vision past a collection of
smaller buildings, stood the Parthenon.

We have no record of Paul's thoughts on visiting ancient
Greece's most storied structure, yet we do know the Athenians of his day revered it more as an architectural wonder than
as a place of worship. They were far more likely to quote Paul
its dimensions, or describe the perfect tilt of its columns than
to sing to him praises of the twenty-two deities decorating its
east pediment or the nineteen gracing its west. They would,
if given the chance, have led the apostle through each of the
ninety-two scenes depicting gods, goddesses, and mythologi-
cal giants in graceful sculpted friezes; yet they would have
brought to the task less reverence for sacred revelation than
their much-heralded zest for a good story.

In a remarkable if roundabout way, from the narrative
of Acts and the testimony of Paul's letters, we know exactly
what Paul thought of Athens. Even amidst its legendary gran-
deur, we know he saw before him not the memory of humankind's golden age but the ruins upon which God's
everlasting kingdom was being built.

> *God has overlooked the times of ignorance, but now demands*
> *that all people everywhere repent because God has established a*
> *day on which the world will be judged with justice through an*
> *appointed man and God has provided confirmation for all by*
> *raising him from the dead.*
>
> Acts 17:30-31

By my last afternoon in Athens, even its history couldn't
hold me. I found myself slipping, with ever-greater regularity,
not into the city's past but into my own. Something had shifted
inside me with the phone call in Thessaloniki; something had

The Agora—Where Paul Sought
to Argue God's Case in Athens

shaken loose in the way I related to events two thousand years before my journey. On this steamy afternoon, in fact, I wasn't relating at all.

As I strolled through two of my favorite Athenian neighborhoods, between the canvas stalls of Monastiraki and past the taverns of the Plaka, I let go of my present completely and retraced two memories of my first visit eighteen years earlier. I did not choose these two memories. The truth is I'd never before thought of them together, for one seemed profane and the other as sacred as any I carried within me. Yet here they were, pressing in upon each other, as though both were longing to occupy the same space. I ducked into a tiny park in the shadow of the Acropolis, seeking out shade to entertain the shadows of my life.

Spring had come early that year, or so the Athenians had told me. Yet they had told me, too, of a winter that nature couldn't drive away: the military dictatorship running the country that had given the world democracy. Many dissidents had been jailed or forced into exile, and many, many in Greece were suffering. I heard of these things only in the briefest whispers, in references to "the way things are now," yet I saw the evidence all around me—a dark subtext to the stones glistening in the clear, spring sunlight.

There he was, day after day, the still-young man in a torn jacket and faded jeans. He tried to speak with me each day as I passed from my hotel through his chosen corner of Syntagma Square. I never stopped to listen, so I built up his full text only after many days of hearing it in pieces.

"My friend," he would always begin, "you are American? Americans are my friends. You are perhaps in your Navy? You are alone here in Greece? I know of a place for you, very nice. The drinks very nice. And many girls, very nice also." By this point I was nearly always out of earshot, but sometimes I heard him say, "If you are alone, perhaps I could take you there. You look, you see. Is okay. You drink, you not drink, is the same."

Is okay. Is the same. Day after day I listened to his pitch. Sometimes he seemed happy with the story he had to tell, other days it seemed to sadden or frighten him. There were days I wanted to laugh in his face: How naive do you think I am? But there were also days when it seemed there was nothing in my life, indeed nothing on earth or in heaven to keep me from accepting his invitation.

"Okay," I said one afternoon, and the sound of my voice almost surprised me.

"It is very near," he said. "You will be very happy as my friends are welcoming you."

The place was just around a couple of corners, but they were corners that took me from the broad sunlit expanse of Syntagma to close, narrow streets full of ragtag offices. I drew a sudden breath and pulled up short when I saw the doorway, a dark hole several steps below the street. I did not move, I could not move, until the young man's grip tightened around my arm and he pressed me down into the hole.

There was music. It sounded American but the lyrics were Greek. All things were suffused with red light, except for pools of ultra-violet that made anything white take on a luminous glow. There was virtually nothing white in the entire bar.

I was seated quickly in a booth off to the side, and I glanced around for the young man without success. When I looked back to my table, I was no longer alone. A young woman had joined me. She was attractive in a tattered Mediterranean way, with far from perfect skin captured in shadow by dark cascading hair. She was smiling.

"You like perhaps some champagne?" she said, then turned to the waiter and ordered some.

"A bottle?" he asked.

But having heard of places like this, I quickly insisted, "No, just a glass." Where had I heard? Oh yes, my father had warned me of places like this. But over the years, I had begun to wonder if I would ever see one. My father had warned me. And now, in this place, I wished I could remember everything he'd ever told me. We toasted with the champagne.

"You know what time it is, don't you?" the woman inquired, and for a moment I started to look at my watch. "No, no," she said. "Not on the clock. In the season. You know, it is the special time. So perhaps you make me some small present?"

She was smiling. Yet her hand had left the stem of her glass and was reaching with palm upturned toward me. I didn't understand.

"It is customary," she said. "You are new here and do not know, but it is very old custom." The hand was almost touching me. "You make me Easter present today? You make me Easter present?"

I jumped up from the table before I could think. "Make your own Easter present," I snarled over my shoulder and bolted for the door. Two large men blocked my exit. "You must pay," they insisted. "For the champagne. For the bottle of champagne."

I paid.

There had never been such a feeling, such a release as I exploded upward from the black cave of the doorway, into sunlight that embraced me. And now, remembering that embrace eighteen years later, I realized for the first time what day it had been. Based on the memory that followed closely, I realized it had been Good Friday.

It was frightening how quickly the second memory tumbled in upon the first, the sacred upon the profane. Didn't these memories realize they had no common ground? Yet there I was the next morning, sipping tea with Cleo in her roof garden and listening to why I should go to the cathedral at midnight.

"It is very special," said Cleo, those gray ringlets flipping across her forehead in the breeze. "I think to say you must go. You would gain much, I think, from going."

Cleo owned the tiny hotel in which I lived that spring. She and I had talked often in this garden: about Athens and its changes, about her childhood as a Greek in Alexandria, about her husband the British officer. The colonel seemed a presence around Cleo's hotel, though she spoke of him with such wistful distance I wanted always to ask his whereabouts. I never asked.

I did, however, go to the Cathedral at midnight. It was only two blocks from Syntagma Square, the briefest stroll from my hotel. Little investment was required, I assured myself, rounding the corner and stepping into a darkened cathedral square. In the diffusion from two huge spotlights trained on the ceremonial doors, I could see that the square was packed. Within minutes, the crowd overflowed into all the streets nearby.

There was a dreamlike quality to the scene that encircled me. There was a hush I had never known among Greeks gathered anywhere. There was an anticipation I had simply never known. And I didn't know why I was there.

Sudden pushing and low whispers alerted me to activity. A long black limousine made its way through the crowd, pulling up to the doors of the cathedral. There was an extended pause, then the limo's back door swung open and a man glinting with military medals stepped out. The huge doors of the cathedral opened. A priest came forth bearing a single candle, whispered a few words to the man in uniform, then watched as he slipped back into his limousine.

The air came to life with murmuring, starting softly yet growing, pushing out into the crowd from the cathedral doors. The darkened crowd began to take on human form as the flame from that candle lit dozens near the doorway, and those dozens lit hundreds more. Everyone around me suddenly held candles, straining forward as a single body toward the light.

"Psst, Mr. DeMers, Mr. DeMers." My name did not even register at first, in the center of all this mystery. But I turned at last and spotted Cleo pushing toward me through the crowd. "Here, Mr. DeMers. You will need one of these."

She pressed a white candle into my hand.

"That was the president in the car," Cleo said. "And that was our archbishop, giving him the news." The news? I could not imagine what the news might be—until the news engulfed me. All around me people were whispering excitedly, one candle lighting another until the flames became a river pouring out into the streets from the square. Cleo accepted a light for her own candle, then reached that new flame over to mine.

"Christos anesti," she said. "Christos anesti, Mr. De-Mers." I stood in silence, still not understanding. "It is Greek language," she explained. "It means: Christ is risen."

I was overwhelmed, shaken to silence by an entire city lighting candles in the darkness, whispering again and again this single proclamation. I could make out the buildings and trees and balconies, all flickering in the votive light.

"Christos anesti," Cleo said again. "Your response is 'Alithos anesti'—Truly he is risen." She smiled, and waited for me to say it.

"Ali-thos," I pronounced slowly, awkwardly. "Alithos anesti."

Eighteen years later, in the tiny park pressed into the side of the Acropolis, I found myself weeping. It was not in sadness or regret, and certainly not in mourning. I wept in something I'd never experienced before, something akin to penitence. I had tried so long to keep my two Athens memories apart but in the end I could not, because they were one memory. I had tried so long to keep my life and faith apart but in the end I could not, because they were one life in faith.

Somehow, I had failed that young woman on Good Friday long ago. I had failed her and a thousand others over the years who had needed me to make their Easter present—to make their Easter present. I longed now to find her and make all things right: somewhere in Athens, somewhere in Greece, perhaps somewhere with God. I knew I couldn't find her. Yet I longed to assure her I was a new person, not the one who had abandoned her. I was a new creation, and I would not abandon her now. I longed to tell her I would make her Easter present. Yes, I would. Yes, I will.

In the light of the candles we light for each other, we must make our Easter present—precisely because our Easter is never past. Christ has died. Christ is risen. Christ will come again. Christos anesti! Alithos anesti!

Ruins of the Temple of Aphrodite
in Corinth

11

CORINTH

The cup of blessing that we bless, is it not a participation in the blood of Christ? The bread that we break, is it not a participation in the body of Christ? Because the loaf of bread is one, we, though many, are one body, for we all partake of the one loaf.
1 Corinthians 10:16-17

Whoever is in Christ is a new creation: the old things have passed away; behold, new things have come.
2 Corinthians 5:17

Thick and green, the serpent stretched across the blacktop road rising from the ruins of Corinth. The snake might have been dead, or simply resting in the already-withering heat of the day, and I was afraid to pass at either end of it. I stood motionless on the melting blacktop, with the near-deafening buzz of insects as background to the slithering sounds of animals among the briars. I glared at the snake in the hope it would move on so I could continue my climb.

There were stories about Greeks and snakes, about how villagers considered these reptiles so evil they beat them till there was little recognizable left. Something scriptural drove Greeks to this violence, some unquenchable anger at the original serpent for costing us the Garden. I had heard of ancient women whipping dead snakes against the rocks until they were nothing but fleshy strings. As I stared at the serpent blocking my path, I would have welcomed the sight of any ancient woman coming toward me along the road.

It was the last full day of my journey in search of Paul, and I was determined to make the most of it, catching a bus out of Athens at dawn, arriving in Corinth hours before my room would be vacant, and jumping onto the first bus out to the ancient city. The entire day shimmered before me with excitement and clarity, for I knew that in just twenty-four hours I would be back in Athens boarding the plane that would carry me home.

Even the news that the ruins were not yet open didn't phase me, despite the awareness of precious hours wasted. I would simply climb along the mountain as far as I could, then head back down to the ancient site. I hadn't counted on the snake.

All alone, surrounded by the fields full of thorns, I realized I was deeply ashamed of my fear. Surely, the snake was dead, though it carried no visible marks of violence or decay. Surely, if it had been alive, it would have sensed my presence and made for cover by now. But it had not budged. In one last attempt at continuing, I pelted the snake with several handfuls of stones. It didn't move an inch.

What was it about this snake? Why did it prevent my progress simply by stretching itself across my path? And why was I so reluctant to pronounce it dead in spite of all the evidence, as though the evil it embodied at that moment could not be counted on to remain dead? Perhaps the Greeks were right about snakes. There would be other days, better days, somewhere in my future to climb the road that ran past Corinth up onto the mountainside.

I returned to the still-silent admission gate, found a shady spot across the road and opened my Bible to Acts of the Apostles. It was time again to find Paul amid the stones of lost centuries, one last time before my journey's end.

Acts tells us Paul's mood was one of dejection when he arrived in Corinth. The entire encounter with Athens had been troubling to him. In Macedonia, he at least had left behind pockets of believers; in Athens, he feared, he had supplied only intellectual amusement. And there was little reason to expect things to be different in Corinth. Paul says he arrived "in weakness and fear and much trembling" (1 Cor 2:3). Yet it does seem the frustrations of Athens had strengthened his commitment. Paul decided to preach in Corinth quite differently, building his arguments not on human wisdom but on spirit and power. "I resolved to know nothing while I was with you," he wrote later, "except Jesus Christ and him crucified" (1 Cor 2:2).

Corinth had not even been on Paul's itinerary, and for a host of reasons it seemed uncongenial soil in which to plant the Gospel. Yet he remained in the city at least eighteen months, longer than he had stayed anywhere since parting company with Barnabas in Syrian Antioch. And he wrote more letters to Corinth than to any other city. Two lengthy ones are preserved for us, reflecting as many as five letters in all. Through his spoken and written word, he molded the Corinthian believers into a large and vigorous young Church.

Paul's establishment of a ministry in Corinth was smoothed considerably, according to Acts, by a Jew from Pontus named Aquila and his wife Priscilla. Owners of a tentmaking firm with branches in several cities, they supplied the apostle with work to support his preaching. Neither for the first time nor the last would Paul use his self-sufficiency as an argument in favor of his gospel. At a more profound level, the fact that Priscilla and Aquila were converts from earlier days in Rome made them key people for Paul to know in Corinth, as well as important links with the Christians of Rome and Ephesus. Later, Paul would write that to Priscilla and Aquila "not only I am grateful but also all the churches of the Gentiles" (Rom 16:3).

The apostle began his preaching in the synagogue, here as elsewhere a place of worship for Jews and God-fearing Gentiles. We are told in some translations that Paul introduced his message by "inserting" the name of Jesus into the appropriate readings, a method that proved persuasive to at least some who heard him do so. These included a ruler of the synagogue known as Crispus and also the Gentile owner of a house next door, identified by the Roman name Titus Justus. When the Jewish authorities decided they had heard enough from Paul, Titus Justus offered his own home to the fledgling Christian community. The residence was the first home of the Church of Jesus Christ in Corinth.

Facing the prospect of a growing new congregation right next door, the rulers of the synagogue sought relief in Roman law. They accused Paul before the proconsul Lucius Junius Gallio of propagating an illegal religion. Today, we wonder exactly what form these charges took: whether they focused on the political implications of the new faith or simply branded Christianity a cult unrecognized by the Roman state. Either way, their arguments had much in common with those offered against Paul in Macedonia. In Corinth, they achieved far less success.

Gallio did not even wait to hear the defense prepared by Paul. He had been sent to Corinth, he declared, to deal with crimes and threats to Pax Romana, not to straighten out theological squabbles among the Jews (Acts 18:12-17). Despite the fact that sooner rather than later Christianity would take on a life quite separate from Judaism, the decision of Gallio allowed Paul to pursue the ministry that would someday make the Corinthians such teaching models for us all.

In keeping with its purpose, Acts shows us little but the steady overcoming of obstacles and the glorious awakening of Corinth to the gospel. Paul's own letters, however, present a more complex picture of his work in this powerful and sophisticated city. We see him struggling to face a profound danger, and facing it only with anguish.

The greatest threat to Christ's Church, he came to realize, was not outsiders seeking to divide Christians, but Christians far too ready to divide themselves. Certainly there were all the familiar adversaries in Corinth—Judaizing "super-apostles" undercutting Paul's authority, and early gnostics promoting an elitist path to knowledge. Yet the issue Paul's correspondence wrestled with most was not error itself but the near-lust of everyday people to embrace it. When even the gifts of the Spirit, given specifically to unite believers by strengthening their faith, when even these gifts seemed to falter amidst "rivalry, jealousy, fury, selfishness, slander, gossip, conceit, and disorder" (2 Cor 12:20), Paul knew he had to speak out or risk losing everything he and the word of God had achieved.

To Paul, each faction in Corinth came to represent a question about Christianity, a question that struck to the heart of its message and its mission in the world. How could this new hope in Christ Jesus transform the earth if the very people who encountered it most passionately disagreed as to its meaning? And how could Jesus' own prayer for unity—so beautifully recalled in John's Gospel—be realized if the very people he prayed for split into parcels of the allegedly saved, and showed little interest in the welcome heaven accorded all the rest?

These were the painful questions Paul labored to answer in his letters to the Corinthians. They were precisely the questions a volatile mix of history and human nature had prepared Corinth to press upon him.

> *When I was a child, I used to talk as a child, think as a child, reason as a child; when I became a man I put aside childish things. At present we see indistinctly, as in a mirror, but then face to face. At present I know partially, then I shall know fully, as I am fully known.*
>
> 1 Corinthians 13:11-12

The peninsula known since prehistory as the Peloponnese seems to dangle from the rest of Greece by a slender thread. This thread, or isthmus, is in actuality an elevated terrace that rises to a rocky hill 1,886 feet above sea level. Ancient Corinth drew its life, its meaning, and its wealth from this terrace and this hill.

Though we lack a specific date for the city's founding, we know it was an important commercial center by the seventh and eighth centuries B.C. At its height, as the leading city of "Greater Greece," Corinth even maintained colonies throughout the region, including the island of Corfu and the city of Syracuse in Sicily. Poets and dramatists such as Pindar, Aeschylus, and Euripedes visited Corinth often and some even made their homes there. Xenophon wrote his "Hellenica" in Corinth, and the Cynic philosopher Diogenes spent many years in the city. To the ancient world, Corinth, when most successful, rivaled Athens in every way. To the Corinthians, who viewed themselves as the perfect mix of intellect and sensuality, Athens was no competition at all.

Though its wealth was generated by location, Corinth's influence rose and fell with the fortunes of war. Corinthian ambitions on Corfu led to the Peloponnesian War in 431 B.C., with the siege of Syracuse ruining Athens and inflicting terrible losses on Corinth. The so-called Corinthian War, in which the city joined with Athens, Argos, and Boeotia against Sparta, weakened Corinth even further. The rise of Philip and the conquests of his son Alexander ended forever the city's dreams of being the capital of the Greek world. Corinth was declared a free city under the Romans in 196 B.C., but its role in leading the Achaean League in revolt led to its destruction half a century later. Its grand buildings were leveled, its men slaughtered, its women and children sold into slavery.

The Corinth in which Paul preached was a new Roman city ordered built by Julius Caesar. This revived Roman colony was actually larger than Athens at that time, suffering from none of its rival's tendencies to be a museum. Corinth wasted little time looking back. It concentrated on its economic and intellectual present in a manner that must have filled the days and nights with incredible vigor. This approach led also to incredible license among its population of Greeks, Romans, Gauls, and North Africans, all serviced by a large population of prostitutes and slaves. To be called a "Corinthian" in Paul's day was to be branded immoral in a major way.

The Marketplace in Corinth
Offered Both Goods and Energetic
Debate

Caesar's rebuilt city prospered, becoming a center of trade and commerce. For a price, ships traveling east or west could avoid the long and hazardous voyage around the Peloponnese by a remarkable overland transfer approximately four miles long. Coming from Asia Minor, Syria, and Egypt, ships docked at the port of Cenchreae on the isthmus' eastern side. From Italy, Sicily, and Spain, they docked at Lechaeum on the west. Either way, cargo was unloaded and hauled across the strip of land, to the opposite harbor and another waiting ship. If they were not too large, even some vessels took advantage of Corinthian engineering, letting themselves be dragged across on a special road called the *diolkos*. Today's Corinth Canal, ordered built by the Emperor Nero but not completed until 1893, is a legacy of the city's importance in Paul's day.

Virtually all structures pointed out to modern visitors were significant to the Corinth of Paul. The Temple of Aphrodite, for instance, is the city's most visible landmark, its seven remaining columns standing stark against the hill called the Acrocorinth. In the ancient world, this temple formed the heart of the sexual license for which the city was famous. The cult of Aphrodite and its one thousand prostitutes found a warm welcome amidst the easy ways of a seaport. Even as the cult faded, its prostitutes had no trouble finding jobs in smaller shrines and, of course, along the docks.

The Jewish synagogue was at the time of Paul's arrival the only haven for Corinthians who resisted the immorality they saw around them. We know from Acts that Jews made up a significant part of Corinth's population. Yet the fact that some of the first to hear Paul's voice in the synagogue were Gentiles reminds us that throughout his travels he encountered all types of people seeking answers in this Jewish center of worship. Archaeologists have identified an inscription among the ruins that reads "Synagogue of the Hebrews." It is almost certainly the synagogue in which Paul launched his mission.

As elsewhere along the Pauline road, the agora formed a central gathering place for the people of Corinth. They bought and sold nearly everything in this marketplace, and they argued tirelessly over politics, finance, or the performing arts. The agora also impelled a major argument into the early Corinthian Church, selling meat that had been sacrificed to idols in the pagan temples. Today, an inscription near the agora contains the same word in Latin (macellum) that Paul used in Greek (makellon) to describe the meat market.

Though the apostle always favored freedom over prohibition, he did see in the debate over whether Christians should partake of "pagan" meat the importance of example. There is no god but God, he knew, and therefore no other had claim upon this meat; yet judgment had to be exercised when it came to others who might misunderstand. "Now food will not bring us closer to God," Paul wrote (1 Cor 8:8-9). "We are no worse off if we do not eat, nor are we better if we do. But make sure that this liberty of yours in no way becomes a stumbling block to the weak."

Excavations have also uncovered a stadium with starting gates for runners, along with temples, a theater, and other buildings used for competitive sports. From as far back as the sixth century B.C., citizens from all across Greece had gathered every two years for the festive Isthmian Games. Though never as famous as the games in Olympia, these were major events, weaving in sports for men and for women, as well as writing and speaking competitions. Paul knew the excitement generated by these games among their thousands of spectators, and he knew the extremes of training endured by competitors to take home a wreath of wild celery. In the dynamics of the Isthmian Games, the apostle found for all ages both a lasting metaphor and a sublime contrast. "They do it to win a perishable crown," Paul tells us of these long-forgotten athletes, "but we an imperishable one" (1 Cor 9:25).

Through the complex daily workings of freedom and responsibility, and indeed of license and discipline, Paul came to understand better the nature of our Christian calling from God. We have the freedom to do all things, he knew from the core of his encounter with Jesus. Yet we have the responsibility to do only things that serve God's children or the Church. As such, our freedom from sin and death securely purchased, we live as slaves to all.

It was this very paradox that Paul hoped to leave as his legacy among the Corinthians when he sailed from Cenchreae for Ephesus. Yet the reports he received there carried him time and again through cycles of joy, concern, anguish, and anger. These emotions may have inspired as many as five letters to the troubled believers in Corinth. The two letters we have, reflecting and perhaps incorporating parts from the others, are extraordinary documents indeed.

We recognize through Paul's encouragements, corrections, and warnings the multitude of dangers Christians face each day. As seen by Paul, at the very heart of these dangers lay a kind of self-satisfaction, a kind of pride in being God's chosen that undermined the power of that very choice.

The grace of God was given more freely than anything the Corinthians could hold in their hands, anything they could win in their stadiums, or purchase in their marketplace; yet once recognized, it seemed to become for them one more proud trophy, one more wreath of wild celery. Valuing only the perishable gifts of their faith—the tongues, the prophecy, the healing—they abandoned repeatedly the unity of their shared loaf and shared cup, the imperishable gift with which and to which God had called them.

> *To this day, in fact, whenever Moses is read, a veil lies over their hearts, but whenever a person turns to the Lord the veil is removed. Now the Lord is the Spirit, and where the Spirit of the Lord is, there is freedom. All of us, gazing with unveiled face on the glory of the Lord, are being transformed into the same image from glory to glory.*
>
> 2 Corinthians 3:15-18

I woke suddenly from a troubled sleep, the terrifying serpent across my path spewing from its mouth the growls of trucks and motorcyles on the street below. Sitting straight up, I worked for several minutes separating my fear on the road above the ruins from the noises of traffic in the night. "It is summer," the man at the desk had warned me, as though at 3:30 on the final morning of my journey that explained everything.

The room was hot and airless, so I flung open the windows and let in still more noise. Night belonged to the eighteen-wheelers, their deep-voiced grindings broken only by short screams from motorcycles and snatches of music escaping from Corinth's waterfront. I was startled by feverish knocking at my door, suddenly certain that someone had come to kill me. But the excited laughter of a young woman's voice made me realize she was knocking for someone else.

In the red glow seeping in from the hotel's neon signature, I found the switch behind the night table and turned on the white light hanging above the bed. An unbearable loneliness crept over me, even with the knowledge I'd be flying home within hours and reaching my family two days before they expected me. I knew I needed to hear their voices, not then but now. I needed to tell them something, not then but now.

Finding the string of codes I'd scribbled down from the man at the front desk, I dialed carefully through each numerical rite of passage—out of the hotel, out of the city, out of the country, then into my own country, my own city, and my own home. I sat at the side of the bed, praying for something other than the abyss that marked the search for a point in the distance as silent as the stars. I prayed for my family, to hear their voices at the end of the line that stretched to the end of God's universe. But there was nothing—nothing!—at the end of the line.

God loves you, I longed to tell my wife and each child. Not just "Home soon," though home soon I would be. God loves you, and so do I!

I was covered with sweat. Perhaps I had been for hours but I noticed it only now. So I surrendered the lifeless receiver, peeled off my clothes, and submitted to an icy shower. There were no towels in my room, so I shook dry as best I could and stripped the top sheet from the bed. Wrapping myself in its caress of pure white, I sat with my Bible at the center of the bed and ventured one last time into the Corinth of Paul.

There was nothing vague about the Corinthians now, nothing distant, shadowy, or historic. Their confusions and errors were no longer exotic to me. They gazed at the world much as I did, and so much of the world they saw caused them pain. They needed Paul, and I knew at last that I needed him, too. Everything seemed to carry promise, yet everything seemed to carry danger. Everything seemed to draw them together, yet everything seemed to pull them apart. Everything seemed to reveal God's presence, yet everything seemed to sweep them headlong into life's floodtide of sin toward death. In that moment, robed in white on that bed in Corinth, the confusions and fears of Paul's Corinthians seemed more overwhelming than any I'd ever encountered—except within myself.

In a world of serpents stretched across our path—some dead, some lying in wait—how do we know how to act? How do we decide what to do? How do we judge the honesty of others and, most importantly, our own honesty? Paul must have searched his heart for the answer, and no doubt searched his life as well. The answer lay buried as deep as that portion of himself that reflected God, as close to the surface as his blood and belief. He had carried the answer since the day of his birth. He had sensed its presence in the light that embraced him in the dust of the Damascus road. Now, for Paul, the fullness of time had been completed. The day had come to give his answer to the world.

If I, he wrote, turning the ultimatum upon himself, if I speak in tongues from heaven and breathe forth prophecies with the voice of God, I am nothing if I speak or breathe with anything but love. If I understand all things and know all things, if I have a belief that overcomes nature, I am nothing if I understand, know, or believe with anything but love. If I walk away from everything I have, and even if I sacrifice my life, I am nothing if I walk away or sacrifice for any reason but love.

Yes, the ages ask with one voice, but what is love? The question was there before him now, unavoidable, stretched across his path as certainly as any serpent. There was no way around it or over it, and no way even to turn and run. What, in truth, is love?

The Greek language of Paul, we are told, had little tolerance for idle thoughts or sedentary emotions, and therefore little interest in describing them. Words that in our tongue mean ideas or feelings have a way, to the ancient Greeks, of meaning motivations with impact. So it is with Paul's love, and so it must be with ours.

Love, he writes, expresses limitless patience and kindness. It does not slip into jealousy or pomposity, selfishness or rudeness. Love never seeks its own reward. It never churns up in anger, broods over injury or celebrates retribution. Love rejoices in the truth—for, of course, the truth is love. It takes on every burden, believes in every possibility, hopes for every good, and endures every suffering. Love, Paul assures us with a simplicity that takes our breath away, never fails.

As with Paul's presence throughout the New Testament, his Corinthian correspondence is an exhortation to embrace the fullness of God's loving news in our lives. We must, in the end, embrace this fullness fully, not only the promised glory but also the present danger, not only the "already" God has given us but the "not yet" we are called to give God. The Corinthian letters are an invitation from Paul—and, yes, from heaven itself—to take into our hearts all the news God has for each of us and arrive at the most important conclusion of all: that it is, beyond measure, news that is good.

Nearly two thousand years after Paul set down the attributes of love and placed it alone at the center of all we hope to offer God, these short sentences penned to the Corinthians remain our single most convincing description of the love God offers us. We do not know what vision, what image, Paul had before him as he described this perfect love; yet the truth is, there could have been only one. No merely human feeling, no merely human emotion, no merely human action in all of history has ever translated this level of sacrifice into what we acknowledge as reality. Only on that single afternoon when God's hand reached out for ours, and only in that briefest of moments when our two hands touched against the wood of a cross, has such love been expressed upon the face of the earth.

Learning to Walk in Paul's
Footsteps

12

BENEDICTION

For I am already being poured out like a libation, and the time of my departure is at hand. I have competed well; I have finished the race; I have kept the faith.

II Timothy 4:6-7

Now to him who can strenghten you, according to my gospel and the proclamation of Jesus Christ, according to the revelation of the mystery kept secret for long ages but now manifested through the prophetic writings and, according to the command of the eternal God, made known to all nations to bring about the obedience of faith, to the only wise God, through Jesus Christ be glory forever and ever. Amen.

Romans 16:25-27

The heat took my breath away. The midday sun burned into me, and it seemed that for a long time there had been no breeze or shade. I had wandered out from the Porta Ostiense, half following the ancient walls and half not caring where I went. I had reached the end of my journey and yet I remained unsettled. Something about the trip seemed incomplete, and melting in the Roman sun I was convinced it would remain that way.

I had not planned to visit Rome at all, despite my longing to explore Paul's final city. No matter how many ways I had twisted and turned my itinerary, Rome simply had not fit. In the end, I had flown out of Athens a day early, hoping to reach my wife and children by Father's Day. I longed to be finished with my journey; I longed to be home. It was with exasperation, then, that I received the captain's message. A passenger had taken ill as we neared the French coast . . . we would have to make an emergency landing . . . we were turning back . . . we had been cleared for an emergency landing . . . in Rome.

My frustration turned to deep sadness when we learned the passenger had died before we could reach the ground. Yet my shock and confusion cleared abruptly when we were handed seven hours to deal with the formalities of his death. I grabbed my passport, exchanged Turkish and Greek currency for Italian, and commandeered a taxi for the Porta Ostiense. The voice of God had spoken! At last!

Still, within two hours of leaving the airport in elation, I knew that Rome was yet another dead end. I felt tired and sad and empty. Most of all, I felt guilty. Guilty for being such an opportunist. Guilty for leaving pregnant wife and three children in the first place. More than anything, I felt guilty that someone had to die to give me Rome, someone I did not know, someone who owed me nothing. In the Roman sun, amid my tormented self-assessments, his all-too-generous gift seemed simply to be melting away.

I had learned many things along the backroads of Paul's missionary journeys, but the value of what I had learned remained a mystery. What good had it done, I asked painfully, to have wandered the streets of Tarsus? What had I gained from standing on the faceless mound of Colossae, or scrambling over the stones of Corinth or Philippi? Paul was not there. Paul was not there! But if not there, if I had not found him in all of this, where was he? And where was I to go?

Before my first steps into this ancient world, I had taken delight in correcting people. "Oh," they said, "you're going to study St. Paul." "No," I countered much too quickly. "I'm going to meet him."

I had wanted to meet him, as crazy as that sounded now in the blinding Roman heat. And for whatever reason, I had not met him. It was as though we'd had an appointment, and he had not shown up. No, not an appointment. A job interview. And now, I realized suddenly, I had trooped through two thousand years of history wishing somebody would take a look at my resume. What a fool's errand! And what a fool!

This was not a conclusion I could live with—not with all the people waiting to hear of my glorious awakenings. Would they accept silent stones? Cities gone without a trace? Stories so crippled that scholars disagree over what they mean, where they took place, and whether they happened at all? Paul would have told me about these things. Paul would have explained his life to me, and maybe mine while he was at it. Paul would have pushed right through the theories and debates, as though they were rain or weariness or sore feet when there was a city to be saved. Paul wouldn't have let me make this journey and somehow still miss the point.

Crazy exhilaration flooded over me at the sight of the archway leading off the street. Shade! It was only an alley between apartment buildings, yet the darkness it framed was irresistible. I stepped out of the sun, stumbling over a pile of crates before my eyes began to deal with the darkness. I could hear water dripping in among the walls, but I was not ready to venture any deeper.

The cool dampness of the alley revived me, and I leaned against a bit of wall, breathing heavily. My eyes focused on the sharp etching of sunlight formed by the archway on the alley floor. The sun did not reach far into my darkness, but its light was intense.

Somewhere in what must have been a maze of alleyways, there was the sound of shifting weight. Something scraped against something else. Something splashed in a puddle, then scurried off with the briefest echo. I turned at the sound, more fearful than I wished to be. And there, amid the shattered wood and refuse, I caught my first glimpse of the apostle Paul.

Flashes of light from the street seemed to carve him for me, just beyond where I could touch, almost beyond where I could see. There was only the barest outline at first, rough and brown, a small man pressed into a corner of the alley.

He might have been a derelict, seeking in darkness no more or less than I was seeking. But I knew he was Paul. And in the strangest awakening of my journey, I knew he had come here for me.

I had traveled so far in search of him. I had studied, I had walked, I had stumbled, I had climbed. Most of all, I had read and reread his words, all we have of the truths Paul spoke to everyone else. In the darkness of that Roman alleyway, I was finally ready to stop traveling. I was finally ready to listen with my heart and let him speak to me.

I, Paul, bring you the grace of freedom here and now, a grace you see each day without truly seeing, know each day without truly knowing. It is the extraordinary gift of an extraordinary God. Yet you live as though both God and the gift are so ordinary. I lived my life that you would not waste your days in such error. Now, in this hour of urgency, the dawn of a new day in God's creation, God sends me to you once again—clothed in all his gifts—speaking again of his love.

Our time together must be short, and there are many things I long to teach you. Some of them are before you already, in what remains of my works and wandering. I pray that after our time together you will never again read them and walk away unchanged. Other things you do not have. They have been lost—as so many of the places have been lost, forgotten and covered over with dust. Still other things you do not have because they are new. They are new born from old in the fullness of time, gifts to you alone from the God who sends me forth once again.

For this journey, God has prepared me well, has given me this body that you might see me, this voice that you might hear me. I have been provided with wisdom to answer the questions you ask even now in your heart. And God has gifted me anew with the places of my life, that we might visit them together and set free your heart in the freedom that is God's gift.

God gives you gifts beyond number, beginning with the gift of life. You are given thought and wonder and truth, faith and hope. God gives you each other and commands that you love, filling you with the very gift that you are asked to give. And God gives you time, a mysterious gift, one you cannot understand until you are beyond its limitations. I tell you, each moment is a precious one; and none is ever so precious as the present one, the one you hold in your hand.

Questions! You have so many questions!

You ask of those who do not know our God, who have not yet thrilled to his presence. There are many in your world not yet blessed with this gift. Together, we must deliver it. It would please me if they hear of God from my lips. It would please me all the more if they hear of God from yours.

You ask of my own people, the children of Israel. You ask if they will ever embrace their Messiah, finding freedom in slavery to their Lord. Today my people again have a home, yet in so many ways they still wander. In abounding generosity, God has granted me the most extraordinary of honors: embracing each of my people as each embraces God's kingdom. They are my brothers and sisters not once but twice, ever in the Lord.

Finally, you ask the most painful question. What of the Christians? What of their errors and cruelties? Their jealousies? What of their failures of courage, their failures of faith, their numberless failures of hope? What, in God's holiest of names, of their divisions? I ask again: Is Christ divided? Who among you truly lives as though we are no longer Gentile or Jew, no longer slave or free, no longer woman or man? Was my preaching not clear enough, not strong enough? Did I, in some way, fail you?

I hear it said there are no simple answers. I tell you today there are only simple answers, and I plead with you to embrace them.

I hear it said that the Churches must learn to talk. Yet the churches have never stopped talking. What the churches must learn to do is listen.

I hear it said that Christ's Church must minister and administer, teach and correct, nurture and defend, instruct and inspire, preserve and console, discern and proclaim. Today, it is even said that the Church must network! Why can't you say the word? Are your lips sealed with clay, your eyes blinded by sand, your heart covered over with stone or ice? The Church must love. The Church must love. The Church must love!

The sunlight was intruding deeper into the alley, its shape lengthening one stone at a time. I drew a deep breath, the first in what seemed an eternity. I watched the little man in the corner, and my heart listened.

There came a day, once again in a Roman prison, that the Lord told me I would not live to see Spain. I was disappointed, for I felt there was much good I might have done there. But then I was told I would not live to see the Lord's coming and vindication among all the peoples of the earth. At this, everything inside me twisted in upon itself to form one terrible scream. Yet my lips could not make a sound.

Room with Mosaic Fragments
Believed to Be Paul's Prison Cell
in Philippi

In the silence, a new fear crept into me, one I had never known—an icy immobilizing fear as I realized that for me, even after all I had endured, all might still be lost. I pressed against the dripping stone wall of my cell, wishing its blackness and emptiness would engulf me. I drew back from the light, as though its slightest touch would be my destruction.

"Paul!"

A voice split open the silence. It seemed louder and more powerful than any I had ever heard, and it was cold and filled with anger. I shivered, for I felt it must be the Lord's.

"Paul! Come forth!"

Fear crippled me. I could not move. I could not speak. I could not breathe. I knew only the sound of that voice, the voice of the one who had come for me. I longed to say, "Lord, I come quickly." But I could say nothing.

The voice grew louder around me and inside me, until it shook the foundations of the earth. I heard the turning of the lock and the heavy iron door swinging open. I turned my face away from the light, shutting my eyes until they burned, pressing myself into the stone.

"Paul! Come forth!" The voice had presence now, a huge shadow filling the doorway. "Come forth. I order you, by the imperial authority of Nero!"

In that moment, in the echo of that word "Nero," I felt a new presence in my cell, a new spirit and a new voice. This was so unlike the voice that had called for me. It was so soft, so impossibly soft, that at first I could not hear it but only knew it was there. It spoke in words that drifted about me, words that when at last I could hear them, I knew suddenly as my own! And yet, hearing them at last in my prison cell, I knew truly they had never belonged to me.

"What will . . ." I heard the voice say. But it drifted away, returning with ". . . the love of Christ." My heart leaped upward into the darkness, grasping for the missing words, longing for ears that could hear them. I heard them then, after a lifetime, spoken haltingly by my own lips. "What will . . . separate us . . . from the love of Christ?"

"Will anguish?" asked the voice, softly and slowly. "Or distress, or persecution, or famine, or nakedness, or peril? Or the sword?"

My voice quivered as my heart caught fire, and I answered God with the words that had been given to me. They cascaded from my lips, faster and faster, beyond anything I had ever known of human speech. "Neither death, nor life, nor angels, nor principalities, nor present things, nor future things, nor powers, nor height, nor depth, nor any other creature. . . ." I drew a long breath, "will be able to separate us from the love of God!"

Now, on this day, I must leave you, passing from all you see as light into all you see as shadow. But on that day, on that glorious day, I stood straight and I stood tall. And I walked, without a limp, out from the shadows of my prison cell, into the blinding light.

I heard his voice with absolute clarity, each word filling my heart with new blood.

I, Paul, called by God to be an apostle and sent forth again in the Spirit, remain a slave of my Lord, Christ Jesus. And now, in my prayers and praises, in my watchfulness and in my love, I am also yours!

John DeMers
in Seleucia
near Antioch